Training and Jobs Programs in Action

TRAINING
AND JOBS PROGRAMS
IN ACTION:

CASE STUDIES
in Private-Sector Initiatives
for the Hard-to-Employ

Researched and Written
by
David Robison

Committee for Economic Development
Work in America Institute, Inc.

Library of Congress Cataloging in Publication Data

Committee for Economic Development.
  Training and jobs programs in action.

    1. Hard-core unemployed—United States.
2. Employees, Training of—United States.
I. Work in America Institute, Inc.   II. Title.
HF5549.5.H3R6   331.1'377'0973   78-7568
ISBN 0-87186-332-4

First printing: May 1978
Paperbound: $5.00
Printed in the United States of America by Georgian Press, Inc.
Design: Harry Carter

COMMITTEE FOR ECONOMIC DEVELOPMENT
477 Madison Avenue, New York, N.Y. 10022
1700 K Street, N.W., Washington, D.C. 20006

WORK IN AMERICA INSTITUTE, INC.
700 White Plains Road, Scarsdale, N.Y. 10583

CONTENTS

INTRODUCTION

NO MORE URGENT ECONOMIC TASK FACES THE UNITED STATES than the achievement of meaningful progress toward high employment without inflation. Yet, it has become increasingly clear that there is little chance of attaining these twin goals simultaneously within a reasonable time without a greatly intensified attack on the structural unemployment problems of those groups that face special burdens which keep them out of the mainstream of the nation's work force. These are the groups that tend to experience unusually high or prolonged levels of joblessness even in relatively good times. They include, in particular, many young people, older workers, and the disadvantaged, especially blacks and other minority groups living in inner cities.

In its policy statement *Jobs for the Hard-to-Employ: New Directions for a Public-Private Partnership* (January 1978), CED's Research and Policy Committee calls for a wide range of public and private actions to deal more effectively with the chronic structural unemployment of these groups. While sound fiscal, monetary, and other economic policies must, of course, be an essential part of this effort, the Committee places particular stress on the need for wider use of direct measures to deal with structural unemployment problems and to strengthen incentives for productive work. Although it recognizes that government programs to train and provide jobs for the hard-to-employ will continue to play an important role in national manpower policy, its main emphasis is on the need for substantially greater private-sector involvement in efforts to aid such groups, both directly and in partnership with government programs.

Private-Sector Programs that Work

Drawing on a special survey of CED trustee companies and a number of other private firms and nonprofit organizations, the Committee concludes that numerous private-sector programs to aid the hard-to-employ already exist and work effectively in various parts of the country. It urges that these programs be used by both large and small business firms as models for much wider use of such initiatives and as a basis for mobilizing greatly increased support for constructive public-private cooperation at the community level.

The case studies presented in this volume represent the results of this survey. They are based in part on responses to a letter that John L. Burns, chairman of CED's Subcommittee on Employment that prepared *Jobs for the Hard-to-Employ*, sent to all CED trustees asking them to describe their own organizations' activities to increase training and job opportunities for the hard-to-employ. The design and scope of the survey, in turn, were an outgrowth of wide-ranging prior discussions within the Subcommittee and with selected representatives of large firms, small business, and labor unions. In light of the many constructive replies to this initial inquiry, CED then commissioned the Work in America Institute, Inc., to explore more fully the experience of CED trustee companies and of a number of other firms and organizations, relying on personal and telephone interviews as well as on written inquiries. David Robison, a staff associate of the institute, carried out this task and was responsible for preparing the individual case studies and the Overview.

The cases cover a wide variety of private-sector activities and public-private partnerships designed to increase training and employment opportunities for the hard-to-employ and speed the transition of the structurally unemployed from government income support and subsidized jobs to permanent private employment. Many of the studies are concerned with special efforts to provide better job preparation, placement, and skill training for severely disadvantaged persons, including those who are undereducated, unskilled, and subject to discrimination or other special handicaps. However, the activities described in this volume are not confined to the disadvantaged. They also include a variety of other ways to reduce the waste that stems from a failure to make the most productive use of the country's total work force. Thus, the cases cover efforts designed to bring about an improved transition from education to work for youths as well as for other age-groups; more productive use of midcareer and older workers, including steps to smooth the transition from regular work to retirement;

wider reliance on part-time work and other alternative work patterns to make more employment available to those youths, homemakers, older persons, and others who cannot conform to a full-time work schedule; and greater business use of alternatives to outright layoffs in recessions, such as skill upgrading and work sharing.

Organizing for a Public-Private Partnership

Jobs for the Hard-to-Employ places special emphasis on the need for more effective organizational mechanisms to mobilize private-sector involvement in programs to reduce structural unemployment. The case studies highlight a wide variety of such arrangements that appear to be particularly promising. These include, among others, direct government manpower contracts with private nonprofit organizations formed by consortia of business firms; reliance on various types of intermediary organizations to help business handle job development, training, and placement activities; jobs corporations and supported-work projects that provide training and jobs for the hardest-to-employ; various cooperative community efforts to aid in the transition from education to work; and a variety of arrangements to establish more effective cooperation between the U.S. Employment Service, government employment programs, and the private sector in aiding the hard-to-employ.

It should be emphasized that the material in the Overview and in the individual case studies is based largely on information obtained from the business firms and nonprofit organizations surveyed. It should not be regarded as an independent evaluation. Moreover, although the case studies include material relating to approximately eighty different companies, they do not constitute a scientific sample and are therefore not necessarily representative of all major firms.

Nevertheless, the studies illustrate the many and diverse types of approaches now being successfully used in the private sector, often in conjunction with various government programs or incentives, to cope with the special problems of the hard-to-employ. No one approach will work for all business firms, communities, or groups. It is to be hoped, however, that this volume will help call much wider public attention to practical private-sector initiatives for aiding the hard-to-employ and will stimulate many firms and communities throughout the country to replicate those programs best suited to their needs. Moreover, as *Jobs for the Hard-to-Employ* indicates, it would be highly desirable if the kind of information presented in these case studies could be made available on a broader and more continuing basis through the establishment of a regular clearinghouse for information on private-sector programs for the hard-to-employ.

Acknowledgments

Many individuals, firms, and organizations helped to make this volume possible. John L. Burns, chairman of the CED Subcommittee that prepared *Jobs for the Hard-to-Employ,* provided the major impetus for the preparation of the case studies.

The Subcommittee and its advisers gave strong encouragement to the project and furnished very helpful information about constructive private-sector initiatives. We are also greatly indebted to the companies and organizations that developed the programs described in this volume and to their officers and staff members who contributed time and effort in providing information and in verifying the accuracy of the case descriptions. Very special credit must go to David Robison for his careful research and perceptive reporting on the various cases. I also want to express sincere appreciation to Jerome Rosow, president of the Work in America Institute, Inc., for his cooperation in supervising the work on this study; to Claudia Feurey, for her invaluable contribution as project editor; and to the Edna McConnell Clark Foundation for its generous financial assistance.

Frank W. Schiff, *Project Director,*
Subcommittee on Jobs for the Hard-to-Employ and
CED Vice President and Chief Economist

OVERVIEW

THROUGHOUT THE COUNTRY, there are already a great many business and community programs that are successfully providing meaningful training and job opportunities for the hard-to-employ. Making these programs more widely known and mobilizing business and community support for them is the key to increasing private-sector participation.

1. ORGANIZATIONAL ARRANGEMENTS

A GREAT MANY PRIVATE-SECTOR ACTIVITIES to assist the disadvantaged and other hard-to-employ groups are carried out through cooperative or unusual institutional arrangements. Some organizations are consortia of companies organized for specific purposes, often to stabilize regional employment and foster economic development or to assist employment of the disadvantaged. In other cases, companies are associated with, or have organized, a nonprofit organization to administer or operate employment and training efforts for the disadvantaged. These private partnerships often obtain federal funds and tend to gain in stability and professionalism as a result of skills that the partnership brings together. In this way, business firms contribute to activities that they might not undertake or sustain by themselves. A nonprofit organization can often provide a professional staff, stable management, and long-term, self-interested commitment to the needs of its disadvantaged clients.

13

Business Consortia

One outstanding business consortium is Chicago United, a multiracial coalition composed of leaders of twenty top companies in Chicago and an equal number of major black and Hispanic businesses. Chicago United emphasizes two themes: cooperation between white and minority business leaders and close business–city government interaction. It is active in economic development, employment, the criminal justice system, public safety and health, education, minority economic development, housing, and transportation.

One of Chicago United's most important innovations is the Chicago Alliance of Business Manpower Services (CABMS). This business-run nonprofit organization, which has a permanent staff, receives Chicago's share of Comprehensive Employment and Training Act (CETA) funds for on-the-job training (OJT) efforts. CABMS organizes, markets, supervises, and contracts directly with Chicago-area employers for on-the-job training. It is a vital intermediate organization that can write an OJT contract within ten days and relieve companies' fears of excessive red tape or regulation by auditing the performance and finances of company OJT contracts. Through CABMS, the city of Chicago has almost quadrupled the number of OJT trainees and the number of employers willing to take OJT contracts within the last two years. Training costs per person were reduced about 15 percent and compare favorably with those of other training programs. In fiscal 1977, CABMS provided 2,776 OJT jobs with 514 employers, primarily smaller employers and minority businesses, at a cost of about $2,600 per job, or $7.1 million. Its principal clients are Chicago's unemployed disadvantaged youths age 26 or under. About 80 percent are members of minority groups. CABMS is administered by the same board and staff as the Chicago Metro office of the National Alliance of Businessmen (NAB) with the executive director of CABMS also heading the NAB office.

Rochester Jobs Inc. (RJI) is a consortium whose directors represent business, commerce, industry, and organizations involved with the poor. Founded early in 1967, it became the Rochester agency of the NAB in 1968. It concentrates on job placement and training activities and administers the Teens on Patrol and World of Work programs initiated by Eastman Kodak Company. From 1967 to 1976, RJI stimulated 16,132 reported hires of the disadvantaged through NAB job campaigns, enrolled almost 10,000 people in employment programs, placed over 6,000 people in training programs, provided 3,400 summer jobs for young people, and aided sensitivity training for approximately 7,000 supervisors through NAB programs.

Another large business and civic group is the Greater Philadelphia Partnership. It was created at the end of 1975 through a merger of the Philadelphia Partnership and the Greater Philadelphia Movement, a twenty-seven-year-old business and civic organization. The new partnership initially sponsored the nonprofit Philadelphia Neighborhood Housing Services, which uses funds from the city and local financial institutions to bring new housing investment into two city neighborhoods. It continues to support the Philadelphia Mortgage Plan, under which local banks have rewritten their lending criteria for old, inner-city neighborhoods; and along with Philadelphia insurance executives, it is currently exploring the possibility of establishing an insurance plan that will increase comprehensive homeowner protection in distressed areas of Philadelphia. It also originated, but is no longer affiliated with, the Impact Services Corporation, which is the supported-work agency for the city.

A group of executives from industry and labor unions, university department chairmen, and community representatives make up the Philadelphia Urban Coalition. In 1970, the coalition, on behalf of the Philadelphia Board of Education, initiated a prototype industrial academy that offers career development for inner-city youths who cannot meet the entry requirements for vocational schools. Known as the Academy of Applied Electrical Science, Inc., it offers a three-year career program in the electrical and electronics fields. Its success in achieving employability for disadvantaged young people and in establishing a bridge between the inner-city schools and industry led to the creation of similar academies in areas such as business and automotive service and mechanics. In addition, the success of these programs inspired an ad hoc committee of industrial executives and the superintendent of the Philadelphia School District to introduce the academies on a larger scale within the Philadelphia school system.

Two other notable business consortia are the 100-member Greater Baltimore Committee, which has led the city's urban renewal efforts, and the Economic Development Council of New York City, Inc., which has been making administrative and project contributions to the city's Human Resources Department, the board of education, schools, courts, and housing programs for over twelve years.

However, the greatest number of business consortia are the NAB Metro offices. There are 120 NAB Metro offices throughout the country. They contact thousands of companies through the services of hundreds of businessmen during NAB's annual job campaigns for the disadvantaged.

Cooperation between Business and Nonprofit Organizations

In many of the cases already described, businesses aid disadvantaged youths or older workers through joint efforts with nonprofit organizations. The business firms provide aid in the form of financial assistance, employment for trainees or members of target groups, training apart from employment, specialized training, educational and career assistance, and professional and business assistance to community groups.

The Training and Technology program in Oak Ridge, Tennessee, is an outstanding example of collaborative effort. One company, Union Carbide, not only provides the industrial setting for training unskilled workers (a nuclear plant) and the instructor-foremen but also hires about one-third of the program's 3,000 graduates. More than sixty other companies hire the remaining two-thirds and provide information on occupational trends. Local governments, using federal funds, pay the training and subsistence costs of enrollees. A consortium of forty-five Southern colleges and universities, Oak Ridge Associated Universities, provides for the program's research, administration, counseling, recruiting, and job placement.

Jobs Corporations

Another form of government-business-nonprofit partnership is the Manpower Demonstration Research Corporation (MDRC), which manages thirteen supported-work projects in cities and states across the country. These projects provide subsidized transitional employment for men and women who have had serious difficulties obtaining and retaining employment. Most MDRC workers perform maintenance, service, security, and housing repair jobs and are gradually introduced to stress, work requirements and assignments, payments, and bonuses by a variety of supported-work techniques. As participants gain work experience, performance demands are increased to prepare them for placement in the conventional job market.

MDRC closely resembles the jobs corporations recommended by CED in *Training and Jobs for the Urban Poor* (1970). In that policy statement, CED proposed an intermediate nonprofit organization that would provide training and jobs for marginal workers and the hard-core unemployed. These people would, in effect, be the corporation's employees. A special feature of the proposal was the partial financing of the corporation through welfare and other public assistance funds that would have been spent on these people if they were not enrolled in such a program.

MDRC is involved in an ongoing study to determine the effects of supported work on the lives of its participants and, with the aid of an independent research organization, to compare them with a matched control group. Through supported-work techniques, MDRC is trying to determine whether four major target groups — ex-addicts, ex-offenders, long-term welfare mothers, and minority youths from low-income families who have dropped out of school — can gain and hold full-time employment in the regular marketplace.

MDRC was established in 1974 with the help of the Ford Foundation; it continues to receive financial assistance from this institution, from five sponsoring federal agencies, and from over 100 businesses and local agencies that contract for the services of supported workers. A total of 5,417 people were enrolled in the program through June 1977, and at least 40 percent of the resources for the projects was provided locally. Government training and demonstration grants and part of the welfare and other transfer payments that participants would have received if they were unemployed also help to support MDRC's work.

Business Interchanges
with State Employment Services

In 1973, an Account Representative program was established by companies seeking to improve their relationship with the Illinois Job Service (IJS). IJS interviewers, assigned to specific companies, received training from company personnel and learned firsthand about specific hiring needs. A close one-to-one relationship developed that strengthened company confidence in the qualifications of applicants sent to them. As a result, employers placed more job orders with IJS and more readily accepted the risks associated with hiring the disadvantaged. Prior to the introduction of this program, IJS's hire ratio was 1 hire for every 18 referrals; after two years with the Account Representative system, the ratio improved dramatically to 1 in 3. Previous placements of 83 people contrast sharply with the more than 2,400 people hired by Chicago companies using the Account Representative system. Over 90 percent of these hires were members of minority groups. Referrals jumped almost five times and placements thirty times.

Recently, the referral functions of the Account Representative system and the system of personal connections between referrers and employers were transferred to the Chicago Metro NAB. A staff of eight people on loan from, and paid by, IJS develop personal relationships with company employment officers, get to know hiring needs, and receive job orders. These orders are forwarded to IJS offices and then to thirty-one cooperating social agencies.

A similar company-employer service exchange has been developed by the Owens-Illinois Corporation in three locations across the country. The Skills in Personnel thru Onsite Training (SPOT) program generates week-at-a-time job trading between company personnel staff and state Employment Service officers. Owens-Illinois is now working with the U.S. Labor Department to make the SPOT program available to more than 100 Owens-Illinois plants across the country and to the local Employment Service offices.

Pennsylvania's Bureau of Employment Security is asking seventy-five employer advisory councils in the state to participate in a similar program. Koppers is one of the Pennsylvania companies that has worked with state employment counselors to acquaint them with the company's requirements for job applicants.

For many years, the Wisconsin State Employment Service maintained a staff of field representatives who contacted Milwaukee-area employers on a monthly basis. That staff was depleted in 1968, but it was recently increased to six employer service representatives. Cutler-Hammer in Milwaukee is one of the companies that encourages this interchange and finds the individualized service a valuable resource.

Self-Help Agencies

Many nonprofit, community-based organizations offer job placement and training services for the disadvantaged, particularly members of minority groups. Probably the most active on a national scale has been the Opportunities Industrialization Centers of America, Inc. (OIC/A). This community-based, self-help employment and skills-training program has affiliates in forty-seven states. It has offered training and job placement to hundreds of thousands of poor and unemployed people since 1964. Local OICs are engaged in recruiting, orientation and counseling, skills training, job placement, and follow-up. A study conducted by General Electric showed that from 1964 to September 1977, 477,000 people had received

OIC training, 280,000 had been placed in jobs, and 85 percent had remained in their jobs after six months. It also showed that OIC graduates had earned $4.8 billion and paid $600 million in taxes and that welfare payments of about $1.5 billion had been saved.

2. IMPROVING THE TRANSITION FROM SCHOOL TO WORK

MANY OF THE COMPANIES SURVEYED by CED feel that a great number of young people come out of school inadequately prepared for the world of work. The consequences are a less productive work force and heavy costs to the economy. Many of these companies are meeting this situation directly by providing supplemental job training and by increasing their support for local school system programs that aid the transition from school to work.

A typical example is the Prudential Insurance Company, which has its corporate headquarters in Newark. Prudential promotes a variety of educational opportunities within the company and in neighborhood schools. The company's projects include support for an alternative school in Newark that helps sixth, seventh, and eighth graders who are unable to cope with the requirements of the regular school system; released time for Prudential employees to tutor remedial classes in elementary schools; a work-study program for students from an alternative school for dropouts that assigns two students to one full-time job; scholarships and employment for students of a predominantly black college; jobs for students of a school for the mentally retarded; and College in the Company, in which Prudential employees teach college courses to both active and retired company employees.

Work-Study Programs

A substantial number of companies have instituted programs that integrate the classroom with the workplace and demonstrate the relevance of education to work. This kind of cooperative education is one of the largest areas of company involvement in training youths.

A leading program is run by the Continental Illinois National Bank and Trust Company in Chicago, which since 1972 has employed about 500 youths between the ages of 16 and 21 in a half-time split between school and work. The program enables the bank to observe these young employees before considering hiring them full time. The student-employees, in turn, gain knowledge about the company's methods and working environment and a clearer idea of job and career opportunities.

Koppers Company has expanded the number of jobs available to co-op students, especially by introducing the work-study concept at smaller company locations. There has been an unexpected beneficial side effect of this program. Koppers's employees working with co-op students learn how to delegate responsibility and at the same time remain accountable for the results of the students' work.

Both Northwestern Mutual Life Insurance and Ralston Purina have work-study projects involving twenty-five to thirty-five high school seniors who work half time at the company and go to school half time. At Ralston Purina, however, the schooling is on site, and the program is geared to students who otherwise might drop out of school.

An unusual work-study system is offered by Texas Instruments in Dallas. Participants work at the company four hours each day and receive financial assistance to attend college engineering classes. (The precise amount of this assistance is determined on a sliding scale related to length of company service and college level.) The project aids young people who lack the economic means to become engineers. About 80 percent of the trainees have been TI employees; the remaining 20 percent are children of employees and youths from the surrounding community.

Philadelphia's high school academy programs (see page 15) have established a realistic bridge between the inner-city school and industry. The Academies of Applied Electrical Science, Business, and Automotive and Mechanical Science offer three-year career development programs for youths who do not qualify for other vocational schools.

Much of the success of these programs can be attributed to business's and industry's involvement in public education. Representatives from business, industry, labor, the school district, and the academic community make up interdisciplinary project teams that supervise the teaching and provide the necessary managerial and technical expertise. Basic skills and the social sciences are taught and related to vocational skills and employability. Industrial and business experiences are provided to supplement classroom instruction. These work-oriented situations allow students to deal with real repair and servicing problems. Joint business-industry efforts also provide both summer and full-time jobs for qualified academy youths.

Career Education

Atlanta's Emory University organized the Developing Interest in Career Experiences (DICE) program to help its students learn about career alternatives while they are studying for their degrees. Business and professional firms in the area act as hosts and offer students four options: career coaching, which provides direct counseling by business and professional people; externships, which enable students to look over the shoulder of a variety of people in a business organization; internships in host companies, which include paid employment; and full-time summer jobs, which include career counseling provided by DICE personnel.

For three years, the Pacific Gas and Electric Company in San Francisco has given twenty of its employees a half day each week to tutor elementary and high school students in the area.

General Electric provides industrial career education for thousands of secondary school educators through its Summer Fellowship and Educator-in-Industry programs. In addition to participating in formal training courses that last from twelve to fifteen weeks, teachers and counselors shadow assigned employees in GE plants and other industries. This exposure to plant work teaches educators technical skills, work practices, wage scales, and employee attitudes. At the same time, it improves their ability to provide practical career counseling to students.

GE also has a variety of programs for young people. The Program to Increase Minority Engineering Graduates (PIMEG) is GE's most extensive career guidance program. (For a fuller discussion of this program, see "Minorities in Engineering," page 38.)

The World-of-Work communications program is GE's way of gearing publicity about career education to student interests. Advertisements that relate hobbies and everyday interests to career aptitudes are placed in monthly scholastic and educational magazines. They emphasize the importance education plays in developing a natural talent. The program also publishes and distributes a series of illustrated job-oriented booklets depicting work. These booklets are updated periodically.

Other GE activities in the World-of-Work program involve teachers, career days, and informative exhibits at educators' conventions.

Vocational Training

Since 1975, Koppers and the state of Maryland have jointly conducted machine shop training, as well as smaller programs in hydraulics and electronics, for three groups of high school graduates in the Baltimore area.

At its refinery at Lake Charles, Louisiana, Cities Service Company helps young people make the transition from school to work through its Employee Candidate program. All applicants for entry-level positions must first complete a five-week program of paid vocational and work aptitude training. Successful graduates become Cities Service employees.

Several programs illustrate business's increasing focus on encouraging minority students to pursue technical training. The Mead Corporation of Dayton, Ohio, offers OJT programs in a broad range of skills at its 140 company locations, including its Southeastern plants, where over 50 percent of new hires are members of minority groups. Certain Mead programs are aimed at recruiting and training special-potential employee groups. The Engineering Co-op program attracts twelve engineering college students each year, primarily those specializing in mechanical and civil engineering. Students work full time with Mead for three months and spend the next three months on campus. They then return to Mead for another assignment.

At Mead's Mulga Mine near Birmingham, Alabama, company managers serve as guest lecturers in mining curriculum at the Walker Technical School. Their goal is to stimulate student interest in mining by exposing the students to actual mining practices and problems. Employees at the mine are encouraged to register for the program under Mead's tuition assistance plan.

INROADS, Inc., which has branches in Chicago, Cleveland, Milwaukee, Pittsburgh, and Saint Louis, wants to reach the gifted poor and help them rise into middle and upper management. Today, 150 corporations sponsor 275 black and Hispanic students for business and engineering careers. Each year, sponsoring companies pay INROADS $1,600 per student to cover the organization's year-round recruiting, counseling, and training programs. About 70 percent of its current graduates are employed by their sponsoring corporations.

Job Placement

In 1976, Vocational Foundation, Inc. (VFI), placed approximately 1,205 of New York City's hardest-to-employ youths in entry-level jobs. VFI is viewed as a youth employment agency of last resort by the 220 New York City social agencies that have referred troubled young people to it. The

majority of these youths have had so
system. VFI is finding job placement
continuing erosion of New York's emp
fierce competition for those jobs that
sates, where possible, by more active
with employers.

Another youth employment servic
twenty years in New York and opened an
in 1977. The Boston office refers job-hun
16 and 21 to employers with entry-level (
placements a month. Both Jobs for Youl ...at they are
especially effective in helping to establis, ..⌣⌣u relationships between
small companies and their young employees.

Summer Jobs

Summer jobs for youths are provided by many companies and local
governments throughout the country and serve a number of purposes.
They provide useful employment and needed income for school and personal expenses; opportunities for young people to understand the world of
work, its conditions and demands, and the career aspects of a given occupation; and special assistance for minority and disadvantaged students.
Summer jobs ease the transition from school to work by providing job
experiences that students can relate to their studies. They also motivate
many students to pursue technical or professional careers. Employers and
their young summertime employees find subsequent full-time job selection easier as a result of their summer acquaintance.

The largest single program of this kind is the summer jobs partnership
of the public and private sectors in Chicago, the Mayor's Summer Program
for the Employment of Disadvantaged Youth (MSPEDY). In 1977, about
85,000 summer jobs were provided, about 46,000 by the city and private
nonprofit agencies and about 39,000 by private companies. The private
sector's summer jobs campaign is organized on an industry-by-industry
basis. Each industry division is headed by the chief executive officer of a
large company whose responsibility it is to write to the top officers of other
companies to solicit their help in hiring youths for the summer.

Members of minority groups gain about 30 percent of the summer
jobs in Chicago's business sector, where no income test is applied, and
about 90 percent of jobs from city and private social agencies, where hiring

is limited to disadvantaged youths. Minority groups represent about 35 percent of Chicago's population. Both the public- and the private-sector summer employment programs have two principal goals: The jobs must be productive, and they must offer the young people opportunities to learn about the world of work. Attitude surveys of MSPEDY job recipients suggest that these programs are meeting their goals and providing badly needed family income and money for school and personal living expenses.

Each year, Ralston Purina in Saint Louis supports summer jobs for about 500 inner-city high school juniors and seniors across the country. They are employed by social agencies and minority businesses for twenty hours each week. Ralston Purina pays the wages and consults with the employers on the work to be done and the type of supervision. Nonprofit organizations, particularly minority businesses, are solicited nationwide to develop the summer jobs.

A combination of the Chicago and Ralston Purina approaches is provided by Westchester County in New York State. The local offices or plants of major corporations and of smaller companies underwrite the salaries of teen-agers working in community agencies. The program is sponsored by Youth Employment Services (YES), a network of twenty-nine local placement and job development services operating year-round in high schools throughout the county. Corporate sponsors have included Avon, Bankers Trust, Exxon, General Motors, IBM, New York Telephone, Stauffer Chemical, and Xerox. Each YES summer job scholarship costs $500. About forty students in each of the past two summers worked in nonprofit agencies such as medical and diagnostic laboratories, a children's hospital, a museum, an art center, and a nature preserve. The program is modeled after a Citibank project started in New York City in 1971 that annually funds up to 140 summer work scholarships with New York community agencies.

Teens on Patrol (TOP), a Rochester, New York, program also focuses on summer jobs for high school students. The program is extremely popular; more than 800 teen-agers apply for the 125 openings. Eastman Kodak Company supports the program by providing annual $100,000 grants, for a total of $1.1 million, to Rochester Jobs Inc., a nonprofit intermediate agency. Since the program's inception in 1966, a total of 1,042 TOP participants have patrolled parks, playgrounds, swimming pools, social centers, and other areas frequented by youths. They ride in patrol cars and do clerical chores at police headquarters. The youths get the feel of police operations and of dealing with the public; in turn, police officers gain greater appreciation and understanding of disadvantaged young people.

A similar program, also funded by Kodak, is the local Sheriff's Teens on Patrol (STOP). Another, funded by Xerox, is Firefighters Involving Teenagers (FIT). Xerox works with Rochester Jobs Inc. and the Rochester Fire Department to place over 300 disadvantaged inner-city youths, ranging in age from 16 to 19. The young people perform all department functions except actual fire fighting. Some thirty-five teen-agers were enrolled in FIT during the summer of 1977.

Like many companies, Alcoa in Pittsburgh hires college students for summer jobs. However, its program is increasingly focused on developing women and minority engineers and business professionals. Some 60 to 70 percent of the 101 students with summer jobs at Alcoa in 1977 were women or members of minority groups.

High School Dropouts

New York City's nonprofit Auxiliary Services for High Schools seeks to help hard-core dropouts and suspended and problem students, all of whom volunteer to return to school. They are taught the basics of mathematics and reading, to learn at their own pace, and to expect promotion when they qualify. Strict discipline and closely supervised work are provided to develop self-reliance and a positive self-image. The program, initiated in 1969, attracts 14,000 students each year. About 2,000 pass the high school equivalency exam, and about 80 percent of these students go on to college.

World of Work (WOW) also aids high school dropouts or potential dropouts. It was started with a $75,000 grant from Kodak in 1970 and a commitment from some Kodak personnel to act as instructors for twenty-five work-study students. Enrollment was increased by 100 students when the project received a two-year Labor Department grant of $1,750,000. WOW is now administered by Rochester Jobs Inc. in cooperation with the Rochester City School District and the Board of Cooperative Educational Services.

During the 1977–78 school year, 230 WOW students will work a maximum of twenty-four hours a week renovating buildings for nonprofit and city agencies and attend classes for five hours on each nonworking day. On the job, the students learn skilled trades (electricity, carpentry, and plumbing) and earn the minimum wage. About 50 percent of these young people have earned high school diplomas or equivalency degrees, and Kodak has hired about 100 WOW graduates.

3. TRAINING AND JOBS FOR THE UNEMPLOYED WITH SPECIAL DISADVANTAGES

MANY OF THE COMPANIES surveyed expressed the conviction that simply providing more jobs for persons with special disadvantages is not the total answer to the unemployment problems of this group. These people need additional help in job-readiness preparation, skills training, education counseling, job placement, and upgrading to enable them to compete and survive in the labor market. A number of companies have found that when disadvantaged people are given enough time, training, and special services, they can advance to the level of other employees.

Between 1968 and 1972, hundreds of companies instituted a variety of special training and employment activities for the disadvantaged. These activities were often part of the Job Opportunities in the Business Sector (JOBS) programs organized by NAB. Both NAB and JOBS were organized in response to an extraordinary conjunction of circumstances and events: the urban riots of 1967 and 1968, the prodding of President Lyndon B. Johnson, and the growing sense of responsibility among American businesses to help to reduce unemployment and racial unrest.

Large-Scale OJT Centers

The 1968–1972 period saw the establishment of large-scale training centers that provided on-the-job training for the disadvantaged. The companies bore the cost of the centers, but training was often partially subsidized by Labor Department funds. Many of these programs were interrupted by the 1974–75 recession and by a hiatus in government support when the administration of CETA funds was shifted to local prime sponsors. A number have been phased out or replaced by other company activities.

Two of the most successful programs were those organized by Inland Steel Company in Chicago and by Chemical Bank in New York.

Inland Steel's MA-6 program employed 520 disadvantaged people who were either unemployed or underemployed and who could not meet normal job standards. Working environments of ten operating departments of the Indiana Harbor Works steel plant were simulated in a vestibule training center set up outside the plant. Company instructors from each department would move back into the plant with their trainees and provide continuing supervision. Training lasted for a maximum of twenty weeks and included instruction in job safety, use of tools and machines, working procedures and behavior, and steel mill terminology. The company was quite satisfied with the job performance of the MA-6 trainees, but the program ended two years later after protracted delays and indecision by the government in renewing another training contract.

Chemical Bank's program lasted from mid-1969 to mid-1974. A professional staff of thirteen and facilities that cost $120,000 per year enabled the bank to offer nine to twelve months of training to each person enrolled. Those accepted were mainly high school dropouts, and almost all were black or Hispanic. Their job-retention rates were not only exceptional (65 to 70 percent after six months of training) but also considerably above those of normal hires.

In the program's latter years, it cost about $500,000 annually (half was covered by federal funding and the other half by the bank) to train from 120 to 180 people per year. This represented about a 50 percent reduction in annual costs and was achieved by improved screening and lower turnover. In the five years of its existence, the program graduated 600 of its 1,000 enrollees. The program ended in 1974.

Other large-scale training activities that emerged in the early 1970s are still in existence but often in revised forms and with new goals. The variety of training programs offered by the 3M Company in Saint Paul is an excellent example. The company opened its Factory Training Center in 1970 to serve hard-core unemployed minority persons. In four years, it trained about 150 people and moved them into factory jobs in Saint Paul. From 1970 to 1971, the center was supported entirely by 3M. Federal funding of $45,000 a year in 1972 and 1973 constituted about one-fourth of the program's total cost. But increasingly, the company's production work moved out of Saint Paul, and the program ended when trainees could no longer be placed locally.

However, 3M has eight other training programs that graduate 300 to 400 people annually. They include an office clerical and key punch OJT program conducted in cooperation with local high schools (in existence from 1960 to 1968); minority on-the-job training and a minority summer employment project; and chemical technician, accounting, college co-op, and summer technical programs.

The Borg-Warner Corporation in Chicago conducted an OJT program for about fifty trainees annually for ten years. In 1977, the total number of enrollees climbed to ninety, with classes graduating in February, May, and September. Trainees learn to operate machines, assemble parts, and cope with the demands of production work. This federally subsidized program costs the government an average of $2,000 per trainee, which is lower than most government OJT grants. However, the program will probably not be continued because Borg-Warner wants to focus instead on upgrading its minority and female employees. The company feels that disadvantaged people can now obtain factory jobs with Borg-Warner through normal hiring practices and with the regular on-the-job training it provides.

The Chrysler Institute in Detroit has been involved in work-study programs and trade skills training since 1931. In 1960, there was a significant influx of disadvantaged and hard-to-employ people into areas of Detroit. The Chrysler Corporation plants responded to this by finding ways to employ these people. With the help of government funds, it developed the Entry-Level Training Department. Realistic training experiences are provided, and the institute seeks jobs for its successful graduates not only in the automotive industry but in other industries as well. Employers report that they find the institute's graduates highly trained and motivated. A large percentage become extremely successful in their careers. Before undertaking a training program in a community, the institute investigates the local job market to identify those occupations that offer the most entry-level job openings. Chrysler has become a leader in the effort to hire, train, and place the disadvantaged and the hard-core unemployed.

Training and Technology (TAT) is highly rated throughout the country and is extremely effective in training unskilled and disadvantaged people for technical jobs. It was founded in 1966 and is administered by the Oak Ridge Associated Universities (ORAU), using a nuclear plant in Oak Ridge, Tennessee, as its training facility. The plant is owned by the government and operated by Union Carbide Corporation. Results show that from 1966 to 1977 TAT placed 96 percent of its 3,003 graduates in skilled jobs at an average 1975–1976 placement wage of $5.59 per hour and that 82 percent of those enrolled graduated.

Many other measures attest to the success and cost-effectiveness of TAT. It is a striking example of a partnership involving government, business, and a group of universities and embodies features that many companies believe are essential to good training programs: strong links to employers, regular surveying of industry's occupational needs, careful screening of applicants, thorough and personalized training, industrial settings, adequate counseling, active job placement efforts, and regular evaluation of the program and its graduates.

RCA is one of the nation's most active companies in the range and scale of its training programs for the disadvantaged. Its five residential Job Corps centers (in Drums, Pennsylvania; Astoria, Oregon; Tulsa, Oklahoma; Marion, Virginia; and Baltimore, Maryland) have a total current enrollment of 1,785 people. The company administers each center and uses federal training funds to support this effort. RCA also operates four other government-financed activities for the training or placement of about 1,200 disadvantaged people. These activities include the Manpower Career Development Agency in New York City, a CETA project in Los Angeles, the Cornwells Heights Youth Development Center School in Philadelphia, and the Cornwells Heights Security Unit School, which is part of a correctional facility for Philadelphia youths.

OJT as Part of Overall Company Hiring Practices

Hundreds of companies provide on-the-job training for disadvantaged persons as part of their total hiring and employment practices. Many are encouraged to do this by the NAB job pledge and hire campaigns conducted in their areas.

One of the most effective private-sector organizations for fostering on-the-job training is the Chicago Alliance of Business Manpower Services (CABMS) (see page 14). NAB's Chicago Metro division, which shares its staff and board with CABMS, is also a leading example of the regional cooperation among companies that support the annual NAB job campaigns. Chicago Metro has consistently led all other NAB offices in both job pledges and job hires. Between 1968 and 1973, Chicago-area NAB companies pledged to employ almost 85,000 disadvantaged individuals and actually hired 103,447 and pledged jobs for 22,500 veterans and hired 19,350. It reported an average job-retention rate of 55 percent after six months, which was comparable to retention rates of regular hires in entry-level jobs reported by other companies.

Among Chicago-area companies, job pledges for the disadvantaged now exceed 36,000 annually, almost as high as the 38,000 pledge level reached in 1973–1974 before the recession. Sixty to seventy NAB executives made personal calls on 3,200 prospective companies in their respective industries during the fall 1977 campaign; their goal was to add 1,700 companies, mostly smaller employers, to the 1,500 already pledging. The Chicago experience suggests that smaller companies constitute the greatest market for expanding the hiring of the disadvantaged so long as the reporting requirements are not burdensome and an organization run by business conducts the job campaign.

The largest training contract among the Chicago companies at any one time was held by Zenith in 1976–1977. Zenith hired 402 disadvantaged persons (92 percent of them minority individuals) for sixteen-week OJT positions paid for by CETA money. CABMS, acting in its capacity as a separate business-run OJT contracting agency, administered the contract and greatly facilitated Zenith's willingness to experiment with a government-funded OJT program.

Although on-the-job training is usually applied to entry-level factory jobs, many companies also use it in specialized fields. In New York, the Vocational Foundation, Inc., joined with a group of engineering and architectural companies to form the Joint Urban Manpower Program, Inc. (JUMP), a program combining classroom and OJT experience in drafting. It enjoyed considerable success until it was discontinued because of the 1975 recession. However, the program was considered so successful in accomplishing its goals that a new JUMP program will begin later in 1978. From 1968 to 1974, San Francisco's Bechtel Corporation trained a total of 145 women and minority group members for entry-level drafting jobs. This program, too, was terminated when the recession hit the construction industry. Northern Vocational Training Company initiated a training program for women in the highway construction trades. Since 1976, under a contract with the Federal Highway Administration, Northern Vocational has trained 120 women a year as highway bridge construction workers, heavy equipment handlers, and off-the-road truck drivers. For ten years, Young & Rubicam in New York has held a government contract to offer a formal training program in advertising skills to the disadvantaged. About eighty-five people have graduated from this one-year course, and thirty-five (about 40 percent) are still with the agency.

On-the-job training has also been used to develop clerical skills for the disadvantaged. The program developed at Levi Strauss in San Francisco allows trainees to learn job-related mathematics, typing, dictation, English, telephone usage, and filing at their own pace and then to apply for permanent jobs with the company. The retention rate is about 80 percent for all trainees and about 50 percent for ex-offenders. Each year, Northwestern Mutual Life Insurance selects twenty to thirty-five (nearly 10 percent of the company's annual hires) for entry-level clerical training. Most are members of minority groups and have below-average academic backgrounds and insufficient skills. Mead Corporation in Dayton, Ohio, is known for the broad range of on-the-job skills training offered in its 140 facilities. About 1,600 (80 percent) of the 2,000 people Mead hires annually are inexperienced, and most are young. In some locations, particularly

Mead's Southern plants, over 50 percent of these new hires are minorities. The length of the training period and the individual nature of the instruction vary according to the type of job. Government support for training is accepted when it is available and can be related to company needs.

Poverty-Area Plants

From 1968 to 1972, a considerable number of new production facilities were deliberately sited in poverty areas. Training needs and start-up costs made many of these facilities unprofitable, and they did not survive their early years. Plants that did succeed were typically backed by a strong company commitment to their survival. Other successful plants were supported by a stable product line and were challenged to meet the same competitive business and production criteria required of other company facilities. Where plants succeeded, community economic stability received a strong boost, and the local work force gained confidence in its abilities.

Control Data Corporation is a leader in siting new facilities in poverty areas. The company's decision to build plants in four economically distressed communities was influenced by a need for added capacity and the belief that a plant in a minority community would tap underutilized human resources. Three of the four locations were selected largely for business reasons: The first plant, Northside, was launched in Minneapolis because the need for employees and jobs was critical and adequate business, technical, and community resources were available. The second plant was sited in Washington, D.C., not only to meet the need for jobs there but because the area had adequate technical resources. The Selby Bindery was located in Saint Paul to provide corporate printing operations. However, the Campton plant was deliberately placed in a depressed Appalachian strip-mining area in Wolfe County, Kentucky, the second-poorest county in the United States. Together, the four plants generate an annual payroll of more than $6.5 million for their communities.

These plants had a combined work force of 840 people as of July 1977. Employment peaked in 1974 at 916 and is moving toward that level for 1978. The decline in employment was part of a marked drop in Control Data's total work force, particularly in production jobs. Technological change in the computer industry, as in many industries, is decreasing labor's input to production.

The IBM Corporation plant in the depressed Bedford-Stuyvesant section of Brooklyn has attained similar success. More than 90 percent of the plant's 400 employees are members of minority groups, and nearly 60 percent were unemployed or working part time before coming to IBM. Eighty-eight percent of the employees live in Brooklyn. According to business measurements that include cost, reliability, quality, and efficiency, the Brooklyn plant is now competitive with other IBM facilities. Employment has been stable, and turnover is about the same as in other IBM plants. However, absenteeism is slightly higher.

In 1970, the Lockheed California Company opened a plant in the Watts-Willowbrook section of Los Angeles to supply assemblies for the L-101 jetliner; it was the largest of six Lockheed plants located in depressed areas. It began with the employment of 243 people and since that time has averaged 200. Some 38 percent of those hired in the plant's first year had criminal records. All received twenty-four weeks of training.

From 1970 (after training was completed) to 1975, the weekly performance of the Watts-Willowbrook work force consistently exceeded the standards used by principal Lockheed plants. The average annual pay of hourly employees increased from $4,680 in 1970 to $12,480 in 1975. By the end of 1975, all supervisory and management personnel except the plant manager were black or Mexican-American. When they were first hired, 90 percent of the plant's employees were on welfare; today, 50 percent own their own homes.

4. OLDER WORKERS

MANY COMPANIES and private nonprofit employers are reexamining their policies concerning retirees and older workers (those over age 40). Although actions have been taken to raise the mandatory retirement age from 65 to 70 years for most workers, the average retirement age is dropping. Only about 15 percent of those age 65 or over are still working. However, the number of part-time older workers is steadily rising.

Reevaluating and Altering Policies

Often, the response of employers to these trends is to institute greater flexibility in work scheduling and work assignments in order to provide a less abrupt transition from work to retirement. Increasing numbers of employers are responding to the needs of their older workers and retirees for job security, adequate pension funds, changes in the pace and responsibilities of work, part-time work, second careers, and review of the economic needs of retirees during periods of inflation. Many companies are changing their pension formulas to minimize the actuarial penalty of early retirement. For example, Northwestern Mutual Life has lowered its early retirement age to 55 for employees who have twenty years of service, with an actuarial reduction from age 60.

In the automobile and steel industries, a policy has prevailed for many years that allows an employee to retire at any age after thirty years of service and receive full pension benefits. These companies have no mandatory retirement age for hourly employees. But because of improved pension and retirement plans, most people in these industries are choosing to retire before age 65.

At Inland Steel, the average retirement age is 59.4 years for hourly employees and 60 years for salaried employees. Only 10 percent of 1976 retirees worked to age 65; less than 0.2 percent of hourly employees are working beyond age 64. This is due in part to the fact Inland has no provision for part-time work. At U.S. Steel, there is no mandatory retirement age for nonmanagement personnel. Older plant and office workers who wish to remain in their regular jobs after they reach the average retirement age may do so as long as their health is judged adequate.

A number of private placement agencies specialize in finding work, most of it paid but also volunteer positions, for older workers and retirees. These agencies include the Federation Employment and Guidance Service in New York; Mature Temps in Chicago and New York; Retirement Jobs Inc., which has expanded to offices in the San Francisco Bay Area and in Cleveland; and Senior Personnel Employment in White Plains, New York.

Part-Time Work

Most of the work available to retirees is part time. In 1970, part-time workers accounted for 14.1 percent of the total civilian labor force; by 1976, the proportion had increased to 14.7 percent. The increase during the same period was significantly greater for older workers. Part-timers 55 years old or older increased from 17.3 to 18.7 percent. In the 55-to-64 age-group, the increase was from 10.6 to 11.7 percent. And for those 65 and older, the increase was from 40.6 to 46.3 percent. It is clear that the work prospects of retirees and those embarked on second careers are closely tied to the growth of part-time work.

The greatest use of part-timers is in the retail trade, where they may constitute 50 percent or more of a particular work force. More than half of the 16,000 employees of Macy's New York division work part time. Macy's has no mandatory retirement age except for executives. Part-time work thus enables many employees and a few supervisors to remain with the company and to adjust to retirement gradually. Of the many employees over 64 who stay on with Macy's on a part-time basis, most do so for about two years.

In addition to the retail trade, opportunities for part-time employment for older workers are prevalent in banking, insurance, fast-food restaurants, supermarkets, transportation, and other service industries.

The program for older workers at the Continental Illinois Bank in Chicago may be the largest of its type. Ten percent of the bank's work force is over 60 years old. An additional 5 percent is 65 or older and has an average tenure of three to four years at the bank; some work even longer. Most of Continental's 440 employees over 65 work part time. The bank has had a policy of mandatory retirement at age 65 but permits its retirees to continue or return as part-timers; they are paid hourly wages.

The bank praises its older workers for their unusual dependability, their seriousness and enthusiasm about work, and their efficiency, which is comparable to that of younger workers. Continental and many other employers report that part-time older workers seem to handle repetitive or low-skilled jobs more readily and with less frustration than younger employees. Of course, older employees want to work because they need the money. But there is more to it than that. They want to be productive and to do a good job.

Prudential Insurance Company employs a great many older part-timers, most of them women in their forties and fifties who are returning to the work force after years as homemakers. Commercial State Bank in Saint Paul hires retirees as customer-service representatives because many of its customers are older people. Connecticut General Life Insurance uses a local senior citizens job bank as a referral source for hiring retirees for short-term work assignments.

However, a number of companies that hire in this fashion avoid using their own retirees because of rigidities in pension and retirement plans. Also, companies are often unwilling to have their retirees come in during overload periods and take on jobs that are lower in pay and status than the jobs of their preretirement years. Union Carbide, for example, cannot hire its own retirees but hires others with appropriate skills and experience that are referred by employment agencies. Cutler-Hammer of Milwaukee uses some of its retired employees as independent consultants on various projects and programs because their familiarity with and knowledge of Cutler-Hammer operations make them a valuable source of service. John Deere Company in Waterloo, Iowa, hired a group of its own retirees as plant guides for visitors because of their long association and familiarity with the company.

A number of companies make special efforts to interview and hire people in their forties and fifties from outside the company. Southwestern Life interviews and hires people in their fifties, but the company's strong internal promotion policy usually leaves only low-level white-collar jobs open to these outsiders.

However, not all part-time work for retirees falls within the lower-paid and lower-skilled categories. Some are highly specialized and well paid. Some of Continental Bank's part-time employees over 60 are specialists who receive officer-level compensation. Kodak, which has flexible retirement, finds that a significant fraction of its part-time work for retirees requires those who are highly skilled.

Some companies make special arrangements for older workers. For example, older workers at Jewel Food Stores are assigned to morning or midday schedules so that they will be able to return home during daylight hours, when the trip is safer for them.

Programs to Prepare for Retirement

It appears that an increasing number of companies are giving consideration to how best to prepare their older employees for retirement. At Prentice-Hall, in Englewood Cliffs, New Jersey, workers nearing retirement age are permitted to scale down their work schedules and responsibilities and move toward retirement gradually. For instance, one year before retirement, a Prentice-Hall employee may shift to a four-day or three-day workweek, with a comparable reduction in income. The company feels that this phased withdrawal permits employees to remain productive while adjusting to growing amounts of leisure time.

Other types of preretirement adjustment programs include IBM's retirement education assistance program, which is unique in that it can be carried over into retirement. Under this program, IBM will pay an employee $500 a year for up to five years to learn a new business or hobby.

The program can be completed before an employee leaves or extended for up to two years after retirement. Because IBM's early retirement age is 55, employees first qualify for this education program at age 52. Mandatory retirement is age 65 for most employees and 60 for corporate officers.

Importance of Income Security

A major component of personnel policies affecting older workers is the extent of job security that a company offers, particularly during recessions. The automobile and steel industries place a strong emphasis on income security, especially for long-service workers. One of the measures taken to protect employee income during layoff periods is relating layoffs to seniority.

IBM is proud of its thirty-five-year tradition of full-employment. During those years, no employee time was lost to layoffs, despite recessions and major product shifts. A major factor in this policy has been the company's ability to shrink its work force by offering older employees incentives to leave. Like most companies, IBM demonstrated this in the recession year of 1975. About 1,900 workers opted for early retirement that year under a special opportunities program that offered liberal benefits: An employee with twenty-five years' service could retire, receive a pension if eligible (reduced pensions started at age 55), and in addition, receive half of his or her annual salary for four years or until reaching age 65.

5. SPECIAL GROUPS
Affirmative Action for Minorities and Women

ALMOST EVERY MEDIUM- OR LARGE-SIZE EMPLOYER has by now developed an affirmative action plan to meet the goals and responsibilities of equal employment opportunity. Private-sector employers have embarked on a massive effort to employ and upgrade women and minority individuals in the nation's work force.

The affirmative action programs of Sears, Roebuck and of AT&T are outstanding in scope, management, and special training programs. Sears, Roebuck, the largest retailer and retail employer in the nation, with a work force of 376,000 people, has a voluntary compliance program whose long-range goals match those of any court-imposed plan. It sets mandatory requirements for groups that are underrepresented in the work force, but it is flexible enough to allow exemptions when these requirements cannot be met. Its implementation system is comprehensive, and it has resulted in rapid proportionate gains for women and minorities in most job categories during the last few years.

AT&T employs the nation's largest private work force (771,000 people) and the largest number of women (401,000, or 52 percent of the Bell System's work force). It developed an affirmative action management system, encompassing its twenty-three operating companies, that is becoming a landmark. The company rectified deficiencies in its first-year (1973) goals and is now meeting its yearly goals by following precise mandated formulas. The system produces 10,800 goals annually. In 1976, AT&T met 99.9 percent of these targets, missing only three. Through its management system, AT&T now knows daily what is needed to meet the goals of every job category in each of its 350 work establishments. The sharpest increases in employment in all categories have been for members of minority groups: from 6.6 percent in 1967, to 13.8 percent in 1972, and to 16.0 percent in 1976.

Special Upgrading for Women

Many employers are developing special in-house training programs to prepare women for high-level jobs. At AT&T, for example, women continue to hold one-third of all management and administrative jobs, and they have made clear gains in moving up into the first and second levels of management. Of the company's 61,000 promotions and new hires in 1976, 39,000 (nearly two-thirds) were women; another 5,000 included men from minority groups. AT&T also has several management development programs that help women make the transition from nontechnical to technical jobs.

Wells Fargo Bank, with headquarters in San Francisco and branches throughout California, provides custom-tailored assistance to women and minorities moving into higher-level positions through its Accelerated Career Development program. Divisional managers identify positions opening up and the leading candidate for each job. After interviews in which the candidate learns what the job involves, he or she submits a self-appraisal that becomes the basis for a training schedule that lists objectives, types of development, and instructors.

Control Data's Selby Bindery in Saint Paul employs seventy-five women for five consecutive hours each morning. This "mothers' shift" allows the women to spend the rest of the day at home with their families. Selby's all-out commitment to part-time employment is especially important to female heads of households and has brought about major savings in welfare costs among its target group of disadvantaged women. The Equitable Life Assurance Society in New York has undertaken at least a half-dozen programs to aid special employee groups, particularly women. The programs involve hundreds of employees and sales agents.

Spanish-Speaking People

In 1969, the Continental Bank instituted satellite recruiting to persuade outer-city and suburban residents to work in the central business district. It believes it was the first large employer in Chicago to do this. Recently, the bank has applied similar techniques to the recruitment of Spanish-speaking people. These techniques include placing recruiting ads in the local Spanish press and radio and setting up temporary offices in Hispanic communities for interviewing. Manufacturers Hanover Trust Company in New York offers in-house courses in English as a second language. There are classes for three levels of language proficiency.

Minorities in Engineering

Analyses have shown that minority groups are significantly underrepresented in the engineering profession and that the number of engineering college graduates from minority groups is insufficient to meet the demands of high-technology companies. This presents a major problem both for companies and for government agencies trying to increase the number of minorities in professional and managerial positions.

In 1973, General Electric initiated the Program to Increase Minority Engineering Graduates (PIMEG); today, there are PIMEG programs in forty-nine GE plant communities. Its purpose is to inform minority young people in junior high and middle school about engineering and to encourage them to pursue it as a career. The program is thus designed to reach students *before* they make critical course selections.

A key feature of the program is the EXPO-TECH trailer, which is equipped with exhibits ranging from simple machines to electronic devices. EXPO-TECH travels to junior high and middle schools.

As efforts to increase the number of minority engineering graduates assumed national proportions, the National Academy of Engineering undertook a leadership role and in 1976 created the National Advisory Council on Minorities in Engineering (NACME). This unique partnership of business, education, government, and the minority community has activated its member organizations to implement local precollege programs for minority students, and more than 100 local NACME programs are under way. These programs identify junior and senior high school students who have potential and interest in engineering, inform the students of opportunities in engineering, motivate parents to be supportive, establish follow-up programs that encourage students during their high school years, and assist students with the funds necessary to carry them into college engineering.

NACME and the National Academy of Engineering helped establish the National Fund for Minority Engineering Students, Inc., which in 1977 provided $2.75 million to assist students in seventy colleges and universities.

Other organizations are participating in this national effort. They include the Committee on Minorities in Engineering, the Minority Engineering Education Effort (ME³), the Negro Academic Committee for Minorities in Engineering, PRIME, Inc. (an outgrowth of PIMEG), and other groups in Atlanta, Boston, Chicago, and Houston.

Training Prisoners and Hiring Ex-Offenders

In Cheverly, Maryland, the Northern Vocational Training Company has graduated over 4,100 trainees who have been released from prisons, particularly the facilities in Lincoln, Nebraska; Lorton, Virginia; Sioux Falls, South Dakota; and Baltimore, Maryland. The company is a wholly owned subsidiary of the Northern Natural Gas Company of Omaha. It estimates that 87 percent of its trainees have been successful in gaining employment and compares this with the national employment rate of 44 percent for those who have been released from prison without work training.

Honeywell Information Systems of Waltham, Massachusetts, first instituted a computer programming course for prison inmates in 1967. Since then, Honeywell has graduated 350 inmates who now work in the data processing field; 300 of them obtained jobs in the computer programming field immediately upon release, and a substantial number found employment in other fields. It currently trains 100 inmates at four Massachusetts prisons; senior inmates are expected to help new trainees. Within the walls of Framingham minimum security prison, eight convicted felons who are serving long-term sentences and who are Honeywell trainees have successfully established an independent company, Con'puter Systems Programming. At least one Honeywell graduate earns $18,000 a year as a systems analyst in the data processing industry. The program boasts a recidivism rate of only 3.9 percent, compared with the state average of 31 percent.

For the past two years, the Borg-Warner Corporation has screened ex-offender job applicants recommended for employment by the Safer Foundation and similar agencies in Chicago. At least fifteen have been hired at the Chicago office. One ex-offender was hired by Borg-Warner as employee-relations coordinator.

In Washington, D.C., the Achievement Scholarship Program, founded in 1973, has offered second-chance educational aid to sixty-four ex-offenders in the form of $700 tuition grants. Five of the awardees have finished their courses, twenty-eight were in school during spring 1977, nineteen have dropped out (many for financial reasons), and eleven have deferred or did not use their scholarships.

Hiring Vietnam Veterans

NAB job campaigns include special efforts to increase pledges to hire Vietnam veterans. One of the numerous companies that have responded is the Standard Oil Company of California in San Francisco. Since 1971, a minimum of 12 to 15 percent of SOCAL's annual hires have been Vietnam veterans. In 1972, a peak year, 500 (about 30 percent) of the 1,700 new hires were Vietnam veterans. In order to facilitate recruiting veterans, all SOCAL job openings are listed with local offices of the Employment Service in communities where the company operates. (SOCAL follows the same procedure to strengthen its efforts to hire the handicapped.)

Hiring the Handicapped

HEW regulations in effect since June 1, 1977, ban discrimination against 35 million handicapped Americans, 10 million alcoholics, and 1.5 million drug addicts. However, many companies, including Sears, Roebuck in Chicago, had already developed programs to aid their handicapped employees. Sears started its program right after World War II but recently reevaluated and revised its policies on accommodating its handicapped employees, especially ways to reduce architectural barriers in its stores.

General Motors Corporation, which has written affirmative action programs in more than 250 work locations, has special hiring programs for disabled veterans and the handicapped in a number of plants. These include a special project for the blind at an Oldsmobile plant in Lansing, Michigan, and a program for the deaf in an Anderson, Michigan, plant.

Eastman Kodak has for some years supported LSW Industries, a wood pallet manufacturer in Clyde, New York, that was founded in 1970 to employ the hard-to-hire and the handicapped. The company presently has sales of $1.9 million and has increased its work force from forty to fifty people. Kodak's Colorado division is the largest customer of sheltered workshops in the area.

Among the private organizations of handicapped workers, Torch Products Corporation, located in several cities, produces light bulbs that are guaranteed for five years; and Just One Break Inc., in New York City, and Abilities Inc., in Albertson, Long Island, function as job placement and training centers.

Employing the Retarded

Since 1967, the National Association of Retarded Citizens (NARC) has developed 20,000 new jobs; annual placements over the past three years have averaged about 5,000. The program is designed to match employable retarded people with specific jobs in industrial and service organizations. Employers provide trainees with a job and 320 hours of on-the-job training. To offset additional training costs, NARC pays 50 percent of the entry-level wage for the first half of the training and 25 percent for the second 160 hours. NARC also sends promotional material and *OJT Information*, a monthly newsletter, to the 2,000 largest U.S. employers.

Westchester Association for Retarded Citizens (WARC) in Westchester County, New York, is rapidly expanding its training and factory centers in White Plains and Mount Kisco. Its work force numbers more than 500 people. WARC's capabilities include wire cutting, drilling, riveting, die-cutting, several types of packaging, collating, and shipping. Contract work has been increasing for the past five years, and industry billings were expected to total about $250,000 in 1977.

Aiding the Educationally Handicapped

Job applicants whose reading and arithmetic skills are at the third to sixth grade levels are being accepted for employment and training by the Cummins Engine Company in Columbus, Indiana. Most of these trainees previously worked at the minimum wage or below, often in seasonal jobs or unstable working conditions. The company's Long-Term Training (LTT) program turns out about thirty graduates annually, providing 10 percent of replacement hires. The company finds that training is the key to turning these people into productive members of the work force. LTT graduates are as successful as regular hires in production work.

6. ALTERNATIVE WORK PATTERNS

THE VARIETY AND USE of alternative work patterns is slowly increasing in the American economy. Departures from the traditional full-time nine-to-five job schedule include flexible hours, permanent or temporary part-time work, staggered hours, job sharing (two people hold one full-time job), shorter hours or a four-day workweek to reduce layoffs, and training or part-time jobs for people on layoff who are receiving unemployment compensation. These options are particularly helpful and important to women returning to the labor force, people with fixed home responsibilities, students, retirees, the unemployed and underemployed, minorities, and workers on layoff.

Flextime

Several hundred large American employers (as well as over 6,000 European companies) are now using flexible working hours. The New York headquarters of the Metropolitan Life Insurance Company provides an excellent example of Flextime in practice. In a survey of Metropolitan Life's supervisors and employees last year, supervisors' evaluations showed positive reactions to Flextime's effect on productivity, employee work habits, administration, and supervision. Employees' evaluations showed positive reactions to time scheduling, use of transportation, and after-work activities. Although Flextime has generally been applied to office, clerical, and service employees, both the Berol Corporation and Hewlett-Packard have extended it to production workers. Many women choose the Flextime option so that they can be at home when their children return from school.

Part-Time Employment

Part-time workers constitute an increasingly large proportion of the American work force. Their employers have found that part-timers do not fit the old stereotypes of marginal, temporary, or uncommitted workers. Part-timers are an increasingly stable work force composed of individuals who want regular work schedules but who also want to work less than full time.

Many employers have instituted permanent part-time work schedules, often where the demand for a product or service fluctuates periodically. Part-time employment is especially widespread in the retail industry; 50 percent or more of the retail work force is made up of permanent and temporary part-time employees. In general, the permanent part-timers have proved to be a stable work force; most are older women with fixed home responsibilities.

Macy's New York division estimates that its two large groups of part-timers (middle-of-the-day employees, who are permanent part-timers and work twenty-five to twenty-eight hours per week, and short-hour employees, who work fewer than five days and often under twenty hours a week) together number over 8,000 people, or just over half of the division's total work force. The store's use of part-timers is crucial to maintaining longer store hours, which are relatively new, and high productivity. The majority of the middle-of-the-day group are women in their forties, many of whom have returned to work after years as homemakers. The short-hour part-timers are mostly students, retirees, and moonlighters.

Other extensive users of part-time employment in the retail industry are Sears, Roebuck, with more than half of its work force made up of part-timers; K-Mart Corporation, with one-quarter of its people working part time; and McDonald's, where 90 percent of the 250,000 employees are part-timers.

Another industry with significant but very much smaller numbers of part-time employees is insurance. At the Prudential and the Travelers insurance companies, housewives and college students work part time to augment the clerical staffs and eliminate some of the need for regular employee overtime and extra pay. Teachers Insurance and Annuity Association and Metropolitan Life also use part-timers to handle peak work loads.

Because of the size of the part-time work force, a number of unions are beginning to organize part-timers. For example, 40 percent of the 700,000 members of the Retail Clerks International Association are part-time workers.

Many manufacturers also employ a substantial number of part-time workers. Among pharmaceutical companies, for example, Upjohn Company has approximately 200 part-timers in its total work force of 18,000.

Another promising use of part-time work is aimed at aiding the disadvantaged. The Selby Bindery in Saint Paul, which is part of Control Data Corporation, employs working mothers in the morning and students in the afternoon. All Selby's employees are disadvantaged, and 90 percent are from minority groups. This employment provides a vital stabilizing force in the community and helps upgrade many of the community's residents to full-time work or further schooling.

The growing practice of employing older workers or retirees on regular schedules of two to three days per week suggests great possibilities for the expanded use of part-timers. Continental Bank offers an outstanding example of this practice. It has shown that employment of retirees and older persons in its Ready Work Force, particularly during the bank's peak work load periods, can provide those people with greatly needed supplemental income.

Job Sharing

A gradually growing phenomenon is job sharing, an arrangement in which two part-time employees divide the duties of one full-time position. By offering many of the traditional advantages of part-time work (shorter hours and flexible schedules), job sharing allows housewives, students, and retirees to pursue careers without jeopardizing other commitments. Often, job sharing includes opportunities not enjoyed by most part-time workers in the past, such as prorated benefits and a prorated full-time salary that is often higher than part-time wages. Some employers have seen a decrease in absenteeism and the need for overtime pay as a result of job sharing. By doubling up during peak work periods or covering for each other during vacations or illness, job pairs minimize the need for temporary help.

A number of nonprofit organizations that offer career counseling and job referral for women are also involved in job sharing. The most prominent is Catalyst, a national network of 181 autonomous women's career centers. Catalyst also issues more than seventy publications and materials on career self-guidance. Within the Catalyst network, the centers most actively involved in job sharing are New Ways to Work in Palo Alto and Focus on Part-Time Work in Seattle, a CETA-funded program.

Work Sharing to Avoid Layoffs

To avoid or reduce extensive layoffs during the 1974–75 recession, all major Western European countries used unemployment compensation to stimulate work sharing. This practice has not been as common in the United States, even though work sharing is approved in over one-quarter of the major union contracts. However, there are some notable exceptions. Inland Steel in Chicago stops hiring when business turns down. Next, it reduces the workweek to a four-day schedule for groups of employees on a two-week rotating basis. Only as a last resort does Inland turn to layoffs. During the worst week of the downturn in Inland's business in the fall of 1975, the company had 1,932 employees on a four-day work schedule and 569 on layoff, out of a total of 18,000 hourly employees who were eligible for the four-day week. Inland points out some of the advantages of work sharing: It keeps crews together; it spreads the impact of a recession and reduces the effect on the individual; and even with a four-day week, the high steel industry wages enable employees to earn a decent income.

A major reason for the use of this practice is that it is permitted under the steel industry's contract with the United Steelworkers. The contract states that in order to avoid layoffs, companies may use the four-day workweek without paying supplemental unemployment benefits. Workers on the shortened schedule are also ineligible for state unemployment benefits.

During 1975, another major example of work sharing to avoid layoffs occurred in the New York Telephone Company, a subsidiary of AT&T. The company presented the union with the choice of either placing 2,000 of its 5,800 New York operators on a reduced workweek or firing 400 of them. The union agreed to the work-sharing proposal.

Work sharing has also been applied in the apparel industry to cope with major fluctuations in demand and at the *Washington Star* in 1975 to avoid a possible closure.

To prevent layoffs of wage-earning plant workers during a business recession, the Chicopee Manufacturing Company, Johnson & Johnson's textile division, implemented several alternative work schedules: the four-day workweek, three weeks working and one week on layoff, and one week working and one week on layoff. The program successfully prevented layoffs during the economic slowdown, and the company was able to return all its employees to full-time schedules.

Relocating and Retraining Workers to Avoid Layoffs

Companies often attempt to relocate their displaced or laid-off workers in other jobs within the organization. For example, in the Johnson & Johnson companies, cutbacks in salaried personnel during the economic slowdowns of 1974 and early 1976 were achieved through a combination of attrition and job matching. Through a clearinghouse established at corporate headquarters, personnel whose jobs were eliminated from economically "unhealthy" companies in the corporation were matched with jobs in "healthy" companies. The job-matching process was done in conformance with affirmative action policies, and the employees placed in new positions received their current salary or the wage rate of the new job, whichever was higher. The process saved 200 positions. The company considers the program valuable and intends to continue to use it when necessary.

Another factor contributing to IBM's full-employment policy is the company's effort to assist employees desiring more than one career. Since 1970, IBM has retrained over 7,000 of its employees and relocated about 11,000. During recessions or shifts of technology or product lines, it tries to move work facilities that have surplus people or to move people to facilities where there is work for them. If those who are transferred lack the skills needed for their new work, they are offered retraining. These practices apply to employees of all ages but are particularly important for older workers whose opportunities to shift careers or locations might otherwise be circumscribed. IBM points out that it is able to offer retraining and relocation because of continued growth in at least one or more divisions at any one time.

In 1970–71 and in 1975, when IBM had an excess of manufacturing personnel, active job placement efforts included describing job openings at employee meetings, having company recruiters travel among divisions to seek applicants for transfer, and at the headquarters level, coordinating measures to balance the manpower for all divisions.

Two IBM programs are geared to the technical revitalization of engineers. Both are voluntary, and participants typically have eight to ten years of service with the company. They receive their previous salaries during retraining and are reimbursed for relocation expenses. General Electric also offers career upgrading and retraining to technical personnel. Tuition for job-related courses is refundable.

Special Assistance
Related to Unemployment Compensation

Occasionally, an innovative system aids workers on layoffs and makes the best use of unemployment compensation. An example is the Learning on Layoff program instituted during the 1975 recession by the Zenith Radio Corporation, with the financial assistance of the Chicago Mayor's Office of Manpower (MOM). Of Zenith's 9,000 hourly employees in Chicago, about 1,000 were on layoffs of several months' duration. The program enabled fifty of these laid-off workers to study basic television electronics, mathematics, reading, writing, and verbal communications while receiving unemployment compensation and retaining their right to recall on a seniority basis. If they were recalled before completing the six months' training provided by the program, they could take educational leave to finish their studies. Forty-eight of the participants were rehired, and four of them were immediately promoted. The company and MOM agreed that Learning on Layoff filled the workers' time productively but felt that more promotions, provided immediately, would have been desirable.

A program developed by MOM and General Electric similarly linked unemployment benefits to training and also provided a few immediate promotions to higher-paying jobs. Both the Zenith and the GE projects cost one-third of other typical government-funded training programs. The reason for this savings was that training allowances, which make up about two-thirds of the cost of a program, were waived because workers were drawing unemployment insurance benefits.

In 1975, American Velvet Company in Stonington, Connecticut, developed another job-saving link to unemployment compensation. The company put its work force on alternating workweeks, and employees were able to draw unemployment benefits during the off weeks.

CHICAGO ALLIANCE
OF BUSINESS MANPOWER SERVICES

Buying Training from Employers

"We buy training, not jobs, although each person has a job from the beginning and may keep it. We give a person a skill. Then that person can compete on his or her own. We buy from employers because who can train better than employers?" That is how Jack Fitzpatrick, former executive director of the Chicago Alliance of Business Manpower Services (CABMS) and now senior vice president for operations for the National Alliance of Businessmen (NAB) in Washington, D.C., explains the essential purpose of the organization's OJT program.

The program's primary target is Chicago's disadvantaged unemployed. The magnitude of the problem it is tackling is enormous. About 80 percent of CABMS's clients are black or Hispanic. And in some areas of Chicago, over 50 percent of minority youths are unemployed, which is twice as high as the rate for white youths.

CABMS is unique in the way it organizes, markets, supervises, and contracts directly for on-the-job training with Chicago employers. It receives funds from the city of Chicago and takes responsibility for writing contracts with hundreds of employers. Thus, the city has to deal with only one organization, CABMS, in order to bring about the largest private-sector-sponsored OJT program in the country. In fiscal 1977, the program provided 2,776 OJT jobs with 514 employers at a cost of roughly $2,600 per job, or a total of approximately $7.1 million.

How the Program Began

CABMS was created in 1972 by Chicago United, the multiracial big-business coalition (see page 57). It became operational in 1975, and it is already showing impressive results.

George Yoxall, manager of personnel and training at Inland Steel Company and a CABMS board member, explains how it developed: "In past years, federal OJT funds were administered by a variety of government agencies with limited success; only a part of the allocated funds was used. There were two major problems: Public agencies made inadequate efforts to market programs to employers interested in OJT, and there were unnecessary delays and bureaucratic red tape. To solve these problems, the Mayor's Office of Manpower (MOM) contracted with CABMS to take over the direct marketing and administration of all OJT contracts with private and nonprofit employers. The initial one-year contract was for 1,000 OJT jobs (300 more than the goal for 1974, when the city ran the program) at a total cost of $4.2 million. CABMS, with the assistance of a major accounting firm, set up simplified, businesslike procedures. CABMS also employed a small number of business-oriented salespersons to market the program.

"It soon became apparent that CABMS would exceed its goal of 1,000 jobs, so MOM raised the total contract to about $6 million for 2,230 jobs.

"All other performance measures have been favorable. Once submitted by employers, the approval time for OJT contracts is now approximately two weeks; before CABMS took over the program, it was several months. Administrative costs are running under 10 percent. The average wage paid to the trainees is higher than in previous years, but the cost per OJT slot is lower. All the trainees were unemployed and met government guidelines, and over 80 percent were minorities."

For fiscal 1977, CABMS maintained its proportion of contracts with minority-owned businesses at about 45 percent, decreased the training costs from $3,000 per slot to about $2,600 per slot, and increased the average hourly wage for trainees from $3.80 to $4.35.

CABMS pays half the costs of the skills training, orientation, and special counseling and pays all the costs of certain brief special supplements (child care, transportation, medical, dental, and meal allowances) until the employee has received a paycheck.

"The reason our costs per placement are going down," Fitzpatrick says, "is that we are writing tighter contracts; we are keeping the training time and costs down to what is absolutely necessary.

"Also, about one-third of the OJT contracts provide for job-related education. In 1976, we offered 100 percent reimbursement for that on the theory that the trainee wasn't contributing anything to the employer. This year, we are paying only half the education cost because we think that education is in the employer's interest, too. We have found that we can market these contracts. That enables us to increase our training capacity somewhat with the same amount of dollars."

How the Program Works

When an employer requests an OJT contract, CABMS checks that the type of job is acceptable. It uses both the Labor Department's *Dictionary of Occupational Titles*, which lists the appropriate training time for each occupation, and MOM's *Manual for Evaluation of the Acceptability of Occupations*. The Labor Department's code allows CABMS to reach a quick decision concerning how much training it should pay for. MOM's manual helps it to determine what occupations are worth providing training for. The manual uses nine factors to rank 430 occupations according to income, education and skill levels, and projected rate of job growth. Many occupations do not pass this evaluation because their education requirements are too high for CETA clients or because their growth rates or wages are too low.

Once proposed OJT jobs are found acceptable and a contract is signed, CABMS helps the employer to find trainees. Referrals may be made to the employer by the Illinois Job Service (IJS) or any of several agencies, such as the Woodlawn Organization, which is run mostly by blacks, and the YMCA. These groups are skilled in prompt processing of job orders, which is important because an employer generally wants applicants within two weeks of the OJT contract's starting date. Trainees may also be preidentified or selected by the employer. CABMS must certify that the applicant is a Chicago resident, has been unemployed for seven calendar days or more, and is new to the specific training and occupation.

Profiles of the Program and Its Clients

A portrait of the OJT contracts, participating employers, and jobs can be drawn from CABMS data covering the six months from October 1976 to March 1977: The majority of the 212 contracts are small; they cover one to five trainees for ten to thirteen months, cost less than $10,000, and involve small firms in which the trainee-to-employee ratio is 1 to 4 or 1 to 3. Almost half the companies are minority-owned. Most are service, manufacturing, and retail businesses. Three-quarters have no more than twenty-five employees. Of 1,122 jobs covering 209 occupations, 258 are professional and technical, 213 are clerical and sales, 213 are in machine trades, and the rest involve structural work, benchwork, and service and processing jobs. An overwhelming number are nonunionized and nonapprentice jobs. Most training lasts three to six months or six to nine months,* costs under $3,200, and involves some orientation, special counseling, and job-related education.

CABMS has also prepared a profile of its first 2,800 trainees from data covering a seventeen-month period ending in March 1977. Most (80 percent) were minorities; the breakdown was 62 percent black, 18 percent Hispanic, and 20 percent white and others. (The population of Chicago includes about 35 percent minorities, 34 percent of whom are black.) The majority (60 percent) were male. Seventy-five percent were at or below the federally set poverty line ($5,800 for a family of four, $4,400 for two, and $3,700 for an individual). In fact, in most cases, being at the poverty level meant that a trainee had not worked during the previous six months. By age, the breakdown was as follows: 20 percent were 21 years old or younger, 70 percent 22 to 45 years old, and 10 percent were over 45. Within that large 22- to 45-year-old group, about half of the trainees were 25 or younger. By educational level, 70 percent of the trainees had not earned a high school diploma, 15 percent had, and 15 percent had more than a high school education.

These statistics demonstrate that CABMS and the employers with which it contracts are serving a very needy group. They are definitely *not* creaming off the most employable job seekers. Jack Fitzpatrick points out that "the nature of the normal, non-OJT hiring process is creaming. Of course, employers will select people who can be most easily trained or who already have skills. That normal process leaves out those without skills. Our applicants and the vast majority of people unemployed for more than ten to twelve weeks don't have any marketable skills."

Clearly, the program's goal of providing on-the-job training to the hard-to-employ who are economically disadvantaged is being met.

---

*The length of the skills-training period depends, of course, upon the job. It may be as brief as nine weeks for a packer or fifteen weeks for a light assembler or as long as forty weeks for an automobile body repair mechanic.

Retention Rates and Terminations

The fact that the majority of OJT contractors are small businesses raises an important question: Is OJT a convenient form of cheap labor? After all, contractors are reimbursed monthly for half the trainee's wages. Do OJT employers hire and fire in recurring cycles?

"The idea of OJT as a source of cheap labor doesn't make sense," says Ray Graham, chairman of the CABMS board and director of equal employment opportunity at Sears, Roebuck. "In the case of a small business, the boss is doing the training. His time is too valuable for him to want to lose trainees."

Kathy Callahan, a CABMS staff officer, agrees: "Small employers want to keep their trainees. Employers tell us that they can't afford to train people only to lose them to other companies because training is a large investment of their time. I know this from the program review reports that we make on site about three times during an average contract, which covers twelve to fourteen months. Furthermore, we weigh retentions as an important factor in considering any future contracts. A pattern of hiring, training, and firing would be obvious. We have found that in cases in which employers have a retention rate of only 50 percent, that rate is often typical of the industry.

"We also get termination reports. We inquire whether the terminations have been positive, neutral (health reasons, relocating, or going into the army or to school), or negative (trainee didn't like the company or couldn't learn the job, absenteeism, poor performance). We find that the reason for a lot of terminations is that the trainee got a better job—for example, better pay in the same field or more responsibilities—moved to a different place, or went back to school."

According to Frank Ickis, who reviews contract performance for CABMS, "about 65 percent of terminations are positive. Roughly, retention and absenteeism rates for our placements are equal to, or better than, those for regular hires. I don't see on-the-job training as cheap labor for small employers. Of our 550 contracts to date, very few have been bad. The vast majority are good contractors, doing the job as intended. This is very important to the success of the program. That's why we keep track, for each one, of retention until thirty days after the end of the contract."

CABMS has found that there is a trade-off between cost savings and adequate retention of jobs. "Any expansion of time and effort invested in a trainee helps," Ickis says. "Counseling in more depth is often important in keeping many employees on the job, particularly during the first six months." Fitzpatrick adds that "the OJT components we build into a job are often so useful that they are instituted by a company for all its employees."

Although its statistical analysis has not yet been completed, the CABMS staff thinks that the overall rate will approximate or surpass the 55 percent retention rate for the first six months of employment found in earlier records of the Chicago Metro office of NAB. Those records for the 1968–1973 period show that Chicago companies hired 103,447 trainees and that 54.9 percent of them were still on the job after six months. Of the 45 percent who did not complete six months of employment, about 25 percent were lost during the first three months and 20 percent during the fourth to sixth months.

Ray Graham says that he doesn't know of "any good studies evaluating what turnover really means. If an employee gets more money at another job, is that desirable turnover or not?"

"Retention isn't the whole issue," Fitzpatrick says. "What is more important is whether the individual is still employed anywhere. Individuals upgrade themselves, blue collar as well as professionals. They can move up, and that makes room in the program for others. Poor people get the skills, then shop around. The assumption that trainees who terminate go back to welfare or unemployment just isn't valid.

"Some employers wring their hands about poor retention rates," Fitzpatrick adds, "but they are generally the ones who don't examine their jobs. Often, the job conditions and pay are poor. One employer admitted that to us: 'We discovered it was a lousy job.' He upgraded salary and working conditions and solved the problem."

In their on-site project reviews, CABMS personnel check not only termination records but also payroll and progress. Then they talk with trainees and watch them on the job. They ask trainees to describe their jobs and what they are learning. Supervisors are also queried. Counseling may be suggested, and employers are informed about problems.

The purpose of this activity is to assure the continuing success of the program. "We may assist the employer," Fitzpatrick explains, "but we aren't an ombudsman. Our contracts are with employers, and we don't make end runs around them."

Key Ingredients of the Program's Success

What makes the OJT process work well? What aspects of CABMS are applicable to other cities? Fitzpatrick cites his organization's twofold strategy: "We control for quality through a careful program design. And we are increasing quantity; we must structurally expand the hiring of the disadvantaged. Five out of six jobs exist in the private sector. Therefore, that is where we must touch more people with what it means to get a job and to work. We must get more businesses involved."

Fitzpatrick lists six key ingredients that have contributed to the program's success: a concerned and receptive local business community; a structure that gets things done (CABMS is separate, nonprofit, yet allied to business, and it can accept CETA funds); an NAB program to foster job pledges and hires that has continuity in planning and operations; a working board of directors with very active committees covering administration, hiring, special target groups, and upgrading; real government-business-labor cooperation (the forty members of the Chicago Manpower Planning Council, which represents these sectors plus client and community groups, meet formally each quarter and almost weekly in subcommittees); and competent staff to formulate plans and carry them out. (To carry out the NAB programs, there are four full-time professionals plus eight others on loan from IJS. To carry out the total CABMS program, there is a professional staff of thirty-five.)

Chicago United, the parent organization of CABMS, plays an important role by providing ongoing support and counsel for all its activities. Chicago United is becoming increasingly active in seeking and implementing solutions to a wide range of urban problems that closely affect the availability of employment and the level of job skills. The organization's access to minority businesses is also essential. In Chicago, 45 percent of the current OJT contracts involve minority employers. At present, twelve of the twenty big Chicago United companies have OJT contracts; in fiscal 1975, under city funding, there were only three. Graham explains that of the eight nonparticipants, several are not hiring, three or four do not accept federal funding as a matter of policy, and several do not want to displace their existing training programs.

Although CABMS and the Chicago Metro office of NAB have the same board and staff for operating purposes, CABMS retains a separate corporate entity in order to preserve flexibility and to be able to contract directly for government funds. Fitzpatrick believes that the lack of an allied NAB vehicle such as CABMS in other cities is one major reason why on-the-job training contracts now receive less than 5 percent of CETA Title I funds. About 25 percent of Chicago's CETA Title I funds are used for on-the-job training. So far, only Cleveland has established a comparable separate organization set up to handle OJT contracts. However, other NAB offices around the country are also seriously considering adopting the Chicago model.

Where CABMS Trainees Go. The job titles shown here are a selective listing of jobs in which fifteen or more CABMS trainees have been employed since October 1975. CABMS estimates that the average hourly wage was $3.80. The average 1977 wage was expected to be $4.35.

JOB TITLE	NUMBER OF TRAINEES	HOURLY WAGES
Professional, Technical, and Managerial		
Administrative assistant	50	$3.00–$9.48
Dental assistant	45	$3.00–$3.50
Store manager	43	$3.10–$6.62
Counselor	42	$3.00–$5.78
Medical assistant	36	$3.00–$3.60
Manager, food services	30	$3.00–$6.50
Social worker	28	$3.00–$5.50
Staff nurse	27	$4.25–$5.91
Legal assistant	15	$4.50–$5.77
Clerical and Sales		
General office clerk	36	$3.00–$5.00
Nurses aide	33	$3.40–$3.50
Stock clerk	30	$3.00–$3.75
Security guard	28	$3.00–$5.00
Janitor	28	$3.00–$3.25
Secretary	26	$3.00–$5.00
Building maintenance	24	$3.00
Insurance agent	21	$4.00–$6.86
Grocery clerk	20	$3.65
Salesperson	19	$3.00–$3.75
Bookkeeper	15	$3.00–$4.50
Machine Trades		
Automobile and truck mechanic	42	$3.00–$7.00
Machine operator	37	$3.06–$4.33
Spindle operator	24	$4.34
Furnace feeder	20	$4.02

JOB TITLE	NUMBER OF TRAINEES	HOURLY WAGES
Processing		
General laborer	20	$5.19
Benchwork		
Line assembler	204	$3.50–$3.96
Dental laboratory technician	78	$3.00–$4.50
Assembler	20	$4.08–$4.22
Structural Work		
Maintenance, factory helper	78	$2.50
Painter	23	$3.52–$4.33
Maintenance person	21	$3.00–$5.20
Automobile body repairman	17	$3.00–$5.50
Miscellaneous		
Mover	36	$3.00–$4.45
Service station attendant	26	$3.00–$4.50
Packer	15	$4.35

CHICAGO UNITED

Multiracial Business Group Works to Counteract City's Jobs, School, and Community Problems

Since 1973, Chicago has been receiving behind-the-scenes business counsel and practical support in confronting its harsh and intractable problems. That help comes from Chicago United, an unusual coalition of twenty of the city's top companies and an equal number of leading black and Hispanic businesses.

Chicago United relies on active participation by the chief executives of these twenty large corporations: Arthur Andersen; Borg-Warner; Carson

Pirie Scott; the *Chicago Tribune*; Commonwealth Edison; Continental Bank; Esmark; Field Enterprises; First Federal Savings & Loan; First National Bank of Chicago; Illinois Bell Telephone; Inland Steel; International Harvester; Jewel Food Stores; Montgomery Ward; Northwest Industries, Peoples Gas; Quaker Oats Company; Sears, Roebuck; Standard Oil of Indiana; and Zenith Radio Corporation. The black and Hispanic leaders represent such organizations as the Chicago Urban League, the *Chicago Daily Defender*, Illinois Service Federal Savings and Loan, Johnson Publishing, Johnson Products, Parker House Sausage, the Woodlawn Organization, Al Johnson Cadillac, Independence Bank of Chicago, Seaway Bank, and the South Side Bank.

This group evolved out of an interracial association of business leaders formed in 1968 after the assassination of Martin Luther King triggered a week of rioting, arson, and looting that destroyed entire sections of Chicago's West Side. By 1971, fifteen white principals were meeting monthly with fifteen minority group leaders. Today, about 140 individuals participate in Chicago United's twenty-five committees and task forces, which tackle concerns that include Chicago's economic development, employment, education, criminal justice system, public safety and health, minority economic development, housing, and transportation. Late in 1976, Chicago United held a series of meetings with experts in each of these areas in order to evaluate the depth of the problems Chicago faces. The experts' reports were made public in March 1977 by the *Chicago Reporter*, a monthly information service on racial issues. The Chicago United evaluation, called "Chicago Report Card," concluded that "for the most part, conditions in Chicago have not improved over the past decade. In most areas they are worsening, and positive action is needed to prevent an acceleration of deleterious trends."*

Robert W. MacGregor, president of Chicago United, explains the overall view: "We felt that Chicago probably does better than other large cities. But all cities are losers. We concluded that the city does have good leadership, resources, and some time left. Chicago works, but a lot of things aren't working. This is especially true of neighborhood deterioration and the outflow of jobs and the middle class."

Multiracial cooperation is one of Chicago United's two main working principles. The other, MacGregor points out, is that "in this city, if you don't work with the city administration, you don't get much done." There-

---

*"Chicago Report Card," *Chicago Reporter* 6, no. 1 (March 1977): 1.

fore, Chicago United emphasizes much closer business-government interaction than most cities, particularly in offering help to the police department, the board of education, and city hall.

Business Development

The "Chicago Report Card" emphasized the city's loss of population to
the suburbs over a decade of cross-migration:

> Chicago lost 500,000 whites and over 200,000 jobs, and gained 330,000
> blacks and 90,000 welfare recipients between 1960 and 1970.

> In the same interval, the suburbs gained 900,000 whites, 500,000 jobs, and
> 350,000 housing units. Chicago's tax base increased by only 24 percent,
> while the cost of living went up about 31 percent. The cost of city govern-
> ment alone increased 60 percent between 1960 and 1970. (p. 8)

The report cited education as the single greatest advantage held by
the suburbs over the city, an advantage that "goes a long way to explaining
the continuous flight of the middle class" (p. 8).
Chicago is financially stronger than other major older cities, but it has
shown signs of weakness.

> Chicago has not been affected like New York City because it handles only
> one-fourth of the functions in terms of dollars that other municipal govern-
> ments handle. For example, Cook County has the responsibility for health
> services, the Board of Education for education, and welfare costs are borne
> mainly by state and federal monies. The Chicago situation looks worse when
> the condition of these separate "governments" is considered. The school
> system . . . has an accumulated deficit of substantially over $100 million.
> The state . . . is in a precarious financial position. (p. 8)

The report anticipated some adaptations but no short-run cures.

> The experts agree that the flow to the suburbs cannot be reversed. Chicago
> interests can only adapt to the outflow, and attempt to retain and attract as
> many productive workers as possible. . . . Many of Chicago's problems
> reflect national trends, and the city cannot do much about them. . . . The
> experts are not optimistic about solutions on a national scale, or large in-
> creases in federal and state subsidies. (p. 8)

Chicago United's most far-reaching effort to keep businesses in the city was to help organize and provide much of the leadership for the new Chicago Economic Development Commission, whose tasks are to retain old industry, attract new firms, and create desirable plant locations. About half of the eighteen commissioners are chief executives who are members of Chicago United. A business development program, funded and organized by Chicago United and prepared by the Fantas Company, specializes in plant siting and helps guide the commission.

Employment and Training

From 1960 to 1970, the city lost about 1,900 plants; during the same period, the Chicago metropolitan area gained about 100. The metropolitan area gained manufacturing jobs between 1963 and 1967 but lost 117,000 jobs between 1967 and 1972. Meanwhile, between 1963 and 1972, the suburbs gained 127,000 manufacturing jobs.

These trends have continued. For example, from mid-1974 to mid-1975, the height of the recession, total metropolitan area employment dropped by 3.6 percent, but manufacturing jobs dropped by 11.8 percent. Between 1969 and 1975, Chicago experienced a loss of 21 percent of manufacturing jobs, compared with a national loss of 9 percent.

These losses may not be permanent. After surveying 100 companies in April 1977, the Economic Development Commission found an 18 to 20 percent increase in employment, which suggests that volatile changes in manufacturing are linked to the business cycle. Nevertheless, in the short run, manufacturing is vital to minority employment. In 1970, about half of the Hispanics and 31 percent of the blacks in the city held manufacturing jobs. Manufacturing has long offered better opportunities for upward mobility for minorities and the lower middle class; their entry into the faster-growing sectors of middle-class jobs and professions has been slow.

Chicago United companies are sponsoring three large-scale job efforts. The most innovative is the Chicago Alliance of Business Manpower Services (CABMS), an affiliate that acts as Chicago United's employment and training agency (see page 49). CABMS receives CETA funds directly from the city of Chicago and writes and handles close to 3,000 OJT positions a year with Chicago businesses. Almost half those contracts are with minority-owned businesses. As a nonprofit organization owned by the Chicago United companies, it is funded by these companies and by government reimbursement of its modest administrative costs.

Some 80 percent of CABMS trainees are black or Hispanic. (Minorities make up 35 percent of Chicago's population.) CABMS follows federal and local guidelines which specify that all trainees must be disadvantaged or unemployed and must be trained in occupations that offer reasonable career chances.

CABMS is expanding rapidly, and its expected placement of about 3,000 trainees in fiscal year 1978 triples its original goal, set in fiscal 1976. CABMS has become the largest private-sector OJT program in the country and is serving as a model for programs in other large cities.

Chicago United's second major jobs program is administered through the Chicago Metro office of the National Alliance of Businessmen (NAB), which has the same board and staff as CABMS. In 1977, the Chicago NAB developed 34,773 job pledges and 36,646 job hires. Over sixty executives participated in its month-long campaign and sold the program to 1,500 Chicago-area companies. This represented an increase of 40 percent in the number of companies reached in 1975.

Its third citywide effort, coordinated through CABMS, is to provide enough summer jobs to meet the needs of most disadvantaged youths. Through the Mayor's Summer Program for the Employment of Disadvantaged Youth (MSPEDY), city and nonprofit agencies will hire about 46,000 youths for the summer, and Chicago United companies will work with other Chicago-area firms to employ another 39,000 youths. The total of 85,000 summer jobs will be the largest number in any one city.

Crime, Police, Justice

Robert MacGregor says that "the number-one concern in this city, according to opinion polls and newspapers, is crime, and it is a primary concern of poor people, of *all* people."

Chicago United's consulting experts reported that between 1971 and 1976, Chicago and the surrounding Cook County had become less safe. During that time, the crime index rose 10 percent in the city and 80 percent in Cook County. Arrests jumped 30 percent in the city and 150 percent in Cook County. The chances of being caught, convicted, and sentenced for committing a felony in Cook County were less than 1 in 100 in 1971; in 1976, they were 3 in 100. The "Chicago Report Card" noted that "this ratio is a major factor in the public's fear of victimization and the justice system's inability to control crime. This fear affects changes in activity plans, decisions about where one lives, business practices and the location of industry." The report also noted a growth of juvenile crime, with more of it handled outside the criminal justice system, and a backlog of 5,379 felony cases in the courts, with an average delay of over 400 days, a heavy dependence on plea bargaining, and a dramatic increase in the number of adults on probation (p. 8).

In response to these findings, Chicago United is working to improve police training and has helped develop a code of ethics for all policemen. It is studying the recommendations of various government and civic groups for court reform and has produced a thirty-minute film on crime prevention that will have approximately 500 showings to employees of Chicago United companies. The film is also being carried on prime-time television in Chicago and other major cities.

Education and the Schools

Chicago United companies have sharply criticized the city's schools because their students have fallen below national averages in academic preparation and because they have failed to equip students with adequate work habits and skills. Chicago United has, of course, been engaged in a number of activities designed to reverse this serious situation.

Chicago United undertook a study of the organization and effectiveness of the board of education, and the board has acted on all the recommendations. The organization's candidate, a bank vice president, has been appointed to the board of education. Chicago United also formed a committee to aid the board in training its administrators. To date, 600 principals and administrators have attended a one-week summer school; additional programs in communications, management, and management systems training are being planned.

A Chicago United committee was commissioned to study career education in the Chicago school system. The committee surveyed twenty chief personnel managers of seventeen Chicago United companies. The report, "Business Views Education in Chicago," was published in *Phi Delta Kappan* in May 1975.

> When asked to estimate the proportion of high school graduates interviewed who are ready for employment with their present educational background, only three respondents felt more than 40 percent were ready. Six said that less than 20 percent of the graduates were ready, and nine said that 20 to 40 percent were ready. Two gave no response. (p. 611)

On the basis of its survey, the Chicago United committee urged two strong work-study recommendations:

1. The schools must provide children with basic skills: reading, writing, spelling, speaking, listening, and computing.

2. The schools must introduce young people to the world of work, so they have reasonable exposure to a variety of career options, and know the amount and kind of training and education needed to reach a career goal. Many businesses are already participating in some form of career education, and are willing to do more. (p. 612)

This Chicago United report spurred the board of education to expand its work-study and career education programs.

A representative of the Mayor's Office of Manpower comments that "job-related experience with education is the most significant thing in Chicago. The student learns about the world of work, which is often completely alien to his family experience. In addition, it provides some income maintenance."

Robert MacGregor adds, "Career education is misunderstood. It is not just vocational education. It encompasses how one learns about work and the thousands of careers available and how students can be exposed to all types of vocations."

A Chicago United committee has considered methods of desegregating the schools. Chicago United and the Chicago Association of Commerce and Industry, the organization that represents the Chicago business community at large, have together selected five members to sit on the board of education's city desegregation committee. The Chicago school system ran out of time in meeting desegregation goals, but the state gave it a probationary period to come up with an acceptable desegregation plan.

MacGregor explains the severity and complexity of the problem: "Chicago is the last major city to tackle this problem. And it could be the most difficult. We have quite a segregated system because of the geography of where the students live. Right now, only 24 percent of the school enrollment is white; it has been declining each year.

"We are very concerned about chasing out more middle-class families, both white and black, to the suburbs. Unfortunately, the whole issue of desegregation seems to accelerate middle-class flight. The city schools are becoming a one-class system, strictly for the poor. Among those enrolled, at least 100,000 kids live in public housing.

"We have to try to keep the Chicago's schools competitive with suburban schools. Many people question spending on middle-class schools; they want more money spent on the poor—and for good reason. But then the middle-class schools decline.

"The whole business community is beginning to become involved in the issue. We have to figure out how to obey the law in this city. All we can do is look at the alternatives. It is largely a class problem. A key issue for all central cities is to keep the skilled-worker and the middle-income families in this city. Business investments are not made in cities populated by unskilled workers. And that has disastrous consequences for the poor.

"We don't yet have an effective strategy to deal with this problem, but Chicago United will continue to address this issue."

Minority Economic Development

Throughout the nation, the value of contracts awarded to minority-owned businesses by firms belonging to the National Minority Purchasing Council doubled in two years, from $237 million in 1973 to $514 million in 1975. Chicago United companies increased their total minority purchases even faster, from $8 million in 1972 to almost $50 million in 1976. The goal for 1977 was to reach $100 million. Chicago United accomplished this by expanding the number of nonmember companies participating in minority purchasing subcouncils, which were divided into industrial sectors.

Phillip Duffy, executive director of the National Minority Purchasing Council, says that the Chicago council is second highest in corporate purchases. "Two of the top five companies in minority vendor purchases are based here," he says, "as well as a high percentage of the top twenty purchasers. A small fraction of the business community is responsible for the $50 million in purchases; a large potential remains untapped.

Chicago United has been involved in a number of other activities to encourage the economic development of the minority community. It has published a guide to purchasing from minority businesses that has been distributed to companies and organizations in forty-one states. Fourteen of the thirty-three regional councils of the National Minority Purchasing Council are using it as a model. Chicago United set up workshops that brought together white and minority banking and insurance firms. These workshops were designed to improve working relationships between the two groups. A reporting system was established, and minority firms noted significant increases in business as a result of these efforts. Chicago United has also presented buyer-information sessions for minority suppliers and majority purchasers in the fields of advertising, construction, printing, and packaging. In addition, the organization has met with construction firms to promote increased minority employment. A twelve-step how-to guide for affirmative action in construction was prepared by Chicago United and distributed nationally.

Housing

Chicago United companies have publicized their support for fair housing and have helped individual employees with housing problems. The organization is also studying revision of the building code and neighborhood revitalization, but in this area, the businessmen are finding it difficult to decide what their role should be.

With the help of a federal grant, Chicago United has also developed an economic plan for the Lower Near North Side that includes recommendations for public housing options. It has helped RESCORP, a for-profit corporation consisting of sixty savings and loan associations who are interested in the rehabilitation of multifamily housing, select the South Shore as the primary target area for their efforts. A Chicago United how-to manual for tenants and homeowners discusses home repairs, maintenance, and budgeting.

Since 1974, one project has combined the organization's interests in youth, jobs, housing, and education. Several hundred youths, all school dropouts, are taught construction skills and paid minimum wages to rehabilitate abandoned buildings in their own community (the Lawndale section) and do other related community improvement projects. Eight gutted buildings, originally purchased for $1 apiece, have been completed at 50 percent less than the cost of building comparable public housing. Unions cooperated in this effort, in part because construction jobs were created by work that the youths could not do.

Closely Interrelated Programs

All the activities in which Chicago United is engaged are vital to doing business in Chicago. "We have just made an internal evaluation of our priorities," MacGregor explains. "First is jobs. Education is the key to jobs. Then we must address public safety because it is critical to where business locates. That leads to transportation. We must have an adequate infrastructure, and that means business development and minority economic development. There are at least six spokes to this wheel, and they are all essential."

An official of the Mayor's Office of Manpower summarizes the city government's view of Chicago United and its role: "Industry has always wanted to be involved in achieving the city's goals and solving its problems. Basically, this has been a happy partnership."

CHICAGO METRO NAB

Job Pledges and Placements for the Disadvantaged

In 1972, Chicago United's Jobs Task Force studied the city's manpower problems and found that the many public and private agencies in the manpower field were poorly coordinated and often working at cross-purposes, particularly in their efforts to get more minorities, the economically disadvantaged, and the unemployed into productive jobs. In addition, the Illinois Bureau of Employment Security was judged relatively ineffective in placing job seekers, irrespective of business conditions and the number of job openings.

One response of the business community was to establish the Chicago Alliance of Business Manpower Services (CABMS), a separate organization that maintains the same board and staff as the Chicago Metro division of the National Alliance of Businessmen (NAB). A second response was to establish the Account Representative program to forge a better relationship with the Employment Service. A third response was to provide more support for the NAB's annual job pledging and hiring activities for the disadvantaged.

Personal Touch

The Account Representative system was relatively simple to organize, but it brought about a major change. Illinois Job Service (IJS) interviewers were assigned to work with specific CABMS contracting companies. They were trained by personnel in these companies so that they learned firsthand about each company's specific hiring needs. Generally, a close one-to-one relationship was established.

The companies gained confidence that appropriate applicants would be sent to them. At the same time, employers gave more job orders to IJS and were encouraged to take more risks in hiring the disadvantaged.

Prior to this program, the Employment Service had a dismal 18 to 1 referral-to-hire ratio with the same companies. In over two years of operating the Account Representative system, the ratio of referrals-to-hires improved dramatically to 3 to 1 and was then maintained at that level. More than 2,400 people were hired in Chicago United companies alone, compared with only 83 placements previously. Over 90 percent of these hires were minorities. Referrals jumped almost five times (from 1,519 to 7,280) and placements thirty times (from 83 to 2,410).

The program was discontinued in August 1976, not for lack of success, but because IJS was without a chief administrator and lacked direction. As of now, it has not been restarted.

Developing the NAB

The referral functions of the Account Representative program and the personal connections between referrers and employers have largely been transferred to the NAB. This has developed gradually as the annual NAB job pledge campaigns have gained increasing acceptance in the Chicago business community.

NAB was formed in 1968, following a White House dinner meeting between President Johnson and fifteen business leaders. The riots occurring in many cities during the 1960s had focused attention on the growing problem of people who were hard to employ.

According to participants, President Johnson asked the businessmen to undertake responsibility for the hard-to-employ and stated that government training programs had been failures, despite the billions of dollars that had been spent on them. The business leaders felt that although the private sector could scarcely handle the whole problem, much greater private hiring might be stimulated. The result was the NAB and its broad effort called Job Opportunities in the Business Sector (JOBS). NAB Metro offices were organized around the country to carry out job pledge and job hiring campaigns.

For most of the period from 1968 to 1973, the national economy was expanding, corporate social responsibility was more closely linked to hiring the disadvantaged, and NAB job pledges and hires by companies increased. This trend was reversed by the 1974–75 recession, during which time even normal entry-level hiring was depressed.

Among Chicago companies, NAB job pledges quickly reached a level of over 25,000 job pledges by 1969. It recovered from the 1970 recession to reach the 25,000 job level again by 1972. With the formation of CABMS and a period of faster economic growth, job pledges rose to 39,000 in 1974. They dropped to 35,000 in the 1974–75 recession and are now recovering above 36,000.

What Is a Job Pledge?

Are the job pledges a numbers game? Or are they matched by job hires? What kinds of hires?

Between 1976 and 1977, there were actually more job hires (36,646) than job pledges (34,773). Of those hires, 73 percent were economically disadvantaged, 24 percent were Vietnam-era veterans, and 3 percent were ex-offenders.

Osceola Edmondson, senior manager of employment and training for Chicago NAB, says that "we tried to address this 'numbers game' criticism in 1976. We didn't try to sell a higher number of pledges to the companies we had previously contacted. We wanted real numbers. We said, 'Tell us what you feel you can actually do.' We told our executives-on-loan, who conduct the pledge campaign, 'It doesn't matter if a pledge goes up or down; stress reachable figures.' In some cases, we talked employers down."

Marie Altieri, who runs the management information system, reports: "A good 75 percent of companies meet their pledges, and about one-fifth of these exceed their pledge; 25 percent don't meet their goal."

Pledging companies report their hires every three months in each of four categories: disadvantaged, Vietnam veterans, summer jobs for needy youths (a separate Chicago program), and ex-offenders. Most people in these categories are, in fact, disadvantaged. The official definition is that the disadvantaged must have a family or individual income below the poverty level or must be unemployed. Also, anyone receiving public assistance is automatically classified as disadvantaged.

NAB is officially limited to these formulas, but it is the companies who must classify and report the numbers. "Many employers try religiously to stick to the formula; others will include all those who need a job," says Jack Fitzpatrick, former executive director of CABMS and now senior vice president, operations, for NAB in Washington, D.C. "Employers try not to embarrass people by probing; some will show the poverty guideline to an applicant and ask if it applies.

"There is little relationship between family income and need," Fitzpatrick adds. "A son may be unemployed and lack any marketable skill; the father can't help on $10,000 a year."

Several years ago, reporting was simplified. Previously, companies were asked to report the number of terminations prior to six months' employment and after six months. Small companies found this reporting especially burdensome; one of their main complaints about government has been red tape.

Also until several years ago, the NAB headquarters in Washington received from each Metro office a profile of job hires by sex, race, income, age, and education. Again, companies found such reporting burdensome, and the NAB, as a voluntary organization, did not wish to insist. Also, with new privacy standards, company application forms generally do not ask for sex, race, and income information.

As a result, the NAB numbers will remain unevaluated. As a whole, though, job pledges do mean job hires.

Filling Job Orders

The regular staff of the Chicago NAB is composed of eight managers of employment and training (METs) who are on loan and are paid by IJS. They have two principal functions: to prepare the annual one-month job pledge campaign and to contact the pledging companies and obtain and refer job orders throughout the rest of the year.

The system is similar to the Account Representative program in that the METs develop personal relationships with company employment officers and get to know their hiring needs. However, METs do not make individual applicant referrals; they send out job orders to any of thirty-one cooperating agencies, especially to Employment Service offices.

Edmondson estimates that IJS will receive 50 to 60 percent of all job orders. IJS will typically get the first chance to fill an order. Often, however, IJS and several other agencies will be asked to make referrals, depending on the employer's location, type of occupation, and number of openings. For example, since many minority or disadvantaged people do not have cars, a suburban job order will be offered to a number of agencies; so will an order for ten or more jobs.

"Most companies want to fill their equal employment opportunity or affirmative action requirements," Edmondson says. "Many will request minority or female applicants. Others will say, 'Vietnam veteran preferred.'

"A pledge only means that a company will try to hire a certain number of people in the next year from the four target groups. It doesn't mean that job orders will be sent solely to NAB or to NAB at all; companies can use gate hires."

Executives-on-Loan

Before the pledge campaigns, METs identify companies to be contacted by using records from IJS, the Chicago Association of Commerce and Industry, and other Chicago directories. The aim is to constantly expand the employer base. In 1976, the number of pledging companies was increased 40 percent from 1,100 to 1,500. In 1977, the goal was to contact an additional 1,700 companies, for a total of 3,200 employers. It was hoped that about half of these new companies would pledge to hire, raising the total of pledging companies from 1,500 to about 2,300.

For the one-month campaign, from sixty to seventy executives are loaned by NAB employers. These are generally middle managers whose salaries, paid by the companies, were worth over $150,000 last year.

The executives are trained for three and a half days, and then each is given a list of about fifty-five companies to contact in the next month. Their goal for 1978 will be to raise the total job pledges above 36,000, mainly by reaching more companies throughout six counties of Illinois and Indiana. "I was impressed with the executives last year," Edmondson says. "It is educational for them: Many say they had no idea that unemployment was as high as it is or as degrading."

As another aspect of the 1977 pledge campaign, the executives visited and briefed 3,000 companies about legislation and affirmative action requirements for hiring Vietnam veterans and ex-offenders. Pledges and placements for these special target groups for 1977 were:

	Vietnam veterans	Disabled veterans	Ex-offenders
Pledges	7,723	619	1,143
Hires	6,608	52	1,060

Obviously, disabled veterans fared poorly. In late summer 1976, NAB held a one-day seminar for over 100 companies to discuss the employability of these groups; it feels that more effort seems needed, especially for the handicapped.

Following Through

After the pledges are signed and the executives return to their companies, the METs begin asking for job orders and referring orders to IJS and thirty-one social agencies. "We don't leave it to the companies," Edmondson explains. "We don't want employers to say, 'We pledged, but you didn't follow up.' Each MET contacts about 175 companies in the first two months after the pledge campaign. Then we take a break and concentrate on companies that didn't pledge, making visits to sell them.

"About 50 percent of our job orders now come in over the phone. We say, 'Give us the job order. Make one phone call to NAB; we will handle it from there, like a broker.'

"We are in competition with the agencies," Edmondson admits, "and everyone is competing with the Employment Service. It is a duplication of efforts, but one that is necessary in a city the size of Chicago and with its volume of industry."

NAB's Record

From March 1968 to March 1973, NAB results were:

	Veterans	Disadvantaged
Total pledging companies . . . 1,519*	652	1,284
Total jobs pledged	22,498	84,826
Total hires	19,350	103,447
Terminations (prior to six months' employment)		46,652
Retention rate		54.9%

* Includes 235 companies pledging for veterans only.

The results show that for the disadvantaged, hires exceeded pledges by almost 19,000 over five years; for veterans, hires trailed pledges by over 3,000. On balance, hires exceeded pledges.

Also, the retention rate of 55 percent for the first six months (a 45 percent turnover) does not seem markedly different from the retention rates that many companies report for regular hires in entry-level jobs. This suggests that the disadvantaged may not be riskier than regular hires, provided that adequate training is given.

The total number of pledging companies for the five-year period, 1,519, is now almost equaled in a single year. This suggests that the NAB's large gains since 1973 have been achieved mainly by expanding the number of pledging companies, rather than increasing the job pledges and hires per company.

For the four years from 1973 to 1976, job pledges totaled 148,906, or an average of 37,227 per year. Hires have averaged about 38,000 per year. By comparison, hires averaged 20,690 per year from 1968 to 1972.

Thus, the Chicago NAB almost doubled its companies' job hires for the disadvantaged and veterans in the last four years, despite the most severe recession since World War II, mainly by reaching out to a much greater number of companies, particularly smaller employers. This is the best NAB record in the country and one that other NAB Metros are being asked to emulate.

OWENS-ILLINOIS

SPOT Program Facilitates Interchange
with Employment Services

In three locations across the country, Owens-Illinois employees and members of state Employment Services trade jobs for one week at a time. Their goal is to understand each organization's needs and resources. The participants' one-week absence from their places of employment is less than the time required for many management development programs. And the only costs to organizations participating in SPOT are employee salaries.

The Skills in Personnel thru Onsite Training (SPOT) program was developed by the U.S. Employment Service and Owens-Illinois in early 1976. Employees from Owens-Illinois plants and from Illinois Job Service (IJS) offices have tested SPOT at the company's headquarters in Toledo, Ohio, in Pittston, Pennsylvania, and in Oakland, California. The company, which manufactures glass, plastic, paper, and metal products, has been so encouraged by the pilot study that it is working with the Labor Department to make the SPOT program available to local IJS offices and more than 100 Owens-Illinois plants across the country.

An IJS representative spends five full days in the plant. Later, one of the plant's personnel staff works in a local office of the U.S. Employment Service. SPOT emphasizes individual development, and most participants report that they did indeed become more familiar with the resources and requirements of each other's organizations.

In a review of the project in *Worklife*, Arthur Swartz, chief of employer services of the Pennsylvania Bureau of Employment Security, states that he plans to extend SPOT throughout the state: "We will ask 75 employer advisory councils . . . if they would like to participate in a program similar to that conducted by Owens-Illinois."*

Peggy Boccolini, employment manager for the Owens-Illinois television products plant in Pittston, participated in SPOT. She says, "I am now using more Bureau of Employment Security services and obtaining excellent results."

In Oakland, Peggy O'Drain fills orders for skilled and unskilled jobs at the local California Employment Development Department. She often handles orders for entry-level jobs at the Owens-Illinois glass container plant in Oakland, which employs 1,800 people. When she spent a week there as a SPOT intern, she received an overview of plant operations, reviewed job descriptions, discussed job requirements with supervisors, and observed workers in action. In the personnel department, she discussed hiring practices, affirmative action plans, employment needs, and job application forms. O'Drain is enthusiastic about the program: "SPOT really gives you a look at private industry. You see what problems employers face. It enabled me to build a very good relationship at the Owens-Illinois plant. Now, when I interview prospective referrals, I try to match the type of job with the type of person. I take more time to explain the type of work and the possible stress involved. I emphasize the need to be dependable, to be a good learner, to have good physical stamina, and to have a reliable means of transportation."

In turn, Willie Huff, a training and equal employment opportunity coordinator at the Oakland plant, worked for a week in the local Employ-

---

*Stephen Brown, "A SPOT of Understanding," *Worklife* 2, no. 7 (July 1977): 27.

ment Service office. He played the role of a job seeker in order to learn how applicants are processed. He also met with the staff to discuss the applicant load and demographics, learned how job orders are taken and filled, practiced classifying local jobs, and learned about the complexities of the unemployment insurance program, the Work Incentive Program, and various youth employment efforts. He also visited two other Employment Service offices in the area. Huff says that he now understands how the Employment Service can help the company meet its affirmative action goals more efficiently, especially through its contacts with community organizations. He thinks that the service can "cut down tremendously" the amount of time he spends developing those contacts himself.

UNION CARBIDE CORPORATION

Oak Ridge TAT Project
Brings Technical Jobs to the Unskilled

In Oak Ridge, Tennessee, a highly effective program called Training and Technology (TAT) has succeeded in placing 96 percent of its previously unskilled enrollees in higher-paying jobs. During the period from 1966 to 1976, 3,003 people completed the program; they constituted 82 percent of all TAT enrollees. The average 1975–1976 placement wage for program graduates was $5.59 per hour.

Many other measures indicate that TAT is both successful and cost-efficient. As a result, the basic TAT program, located in Oak Ridge at the government-owned Y-12 nuclear plant operated by the Union Carbide Corporation, is being adapted at several other locations across the country. Organizers hope to replicate TAT's effectiveness in training the unskilled for technical jobs.

Most TAT trainees are referred by Tennessee CETA prime sponsors (local governments disbursing federal employment and training funds). Until 1974, the target group was the disadvantaged. At present, the targets are the unemployed and the underemployed, but most of the trainees are also disadvantaged. In recent years, an average of 63 percent of the trainees were previously unemployed. Through 1973, 65 to 75 percent were disadvantaged, which meant that they met the Labor Department's definition by being poor, lacking suitable employment, and being under 22 or over 45 years old, a member of a minority group, a school dropout, or handicapped. Another group that qualified was high school graduates who were underemployed; these were teen-agers who were working in low-skilled, dead-end jobs.

About 68 percent of the trainees have been white; 31 percent, black; and 1 percent, others. The proportion of blacks is high compared with the proportion of blacks in the surrounding areas (7 percent). About 87 percent of the applicants were Tennessee residents, although recruitment covered a wider area. About 13 percent have been women; previously, the proportion was 7 percent. Most of the trainees are young. The average age is 22, and about 90 percent are under 25. However, TAT trainees overall range in age from 17 to 54.

Factory Setting

TAT trainees enter the plant gates at the same time and with the same badges as other workers. They are subject to the same plant rules and discipline. Their instructors, who are Union Carbide foremen, accept or reject their shopwork according to strict industrial standards. Jack Fritts, head of the program, says, "The standards we impose are the ones that industry expects from its employees. They are much more stringent than the standards in most vocational schools."

According to a 1973 Labor Department report, the program's "industrial setting is a prime ingredient of training success." It helps to motivate the trainees and to keep them in the program. (Only 18 percent of enrollees fail to graduate from TAT.) The factory setting also encourages "the formation of work habits that will prepare graduates for the real obligations of employment". * These work habits include, among other things, punctuality and good attendance. For example, after six unexcused absences, a trainee is fired.

During their six months in the program, trainees spend forty hours each week at the plant, mostly in hands-on use of advanced production equipment in shops and laboratories. An average of eleven hours a week are devoted to classes (five hours of mathematics, three hours of science,

---

*U.S. Department of Labor, *A Model for Training the Disadvantaged: TAT at Oak Ridge, Tenn.*, Manpower Research Monograph no. 29, 1973.

and two hours of blueprint reading). Double shifts in machining, welding and physical testing keep the facility open from 7 A.M. to 11 P.M.

The job skills taught are either those generally in demand in technology-based industries and construction or those specifically required by employers hiring TAT graduates. Currently, five training areas are offered: machining, welding, drafting technology, physical testing, and mechanical operations (pipe fitting, hydraulics, and the like). Previous courses included industrial electricity, glassblowing, machine shop inspection, electronics, and training for chemical technicians. When the demand for these skills declined, the courses were phased out.

TAT also provides a wide range of supportive services, including help in locating housing, transportation, and recreation and assistance in coping with personal, medical, and financial problems.

A High Level of Success

TAT is known for its ability to deliver good jobs for its trainees, and the program attracts up to ten applicants for each opening. TAT actively recruits through schools, churches, the employment service, and the local media.

The Labor Department's review identified the elements that contribute to TAT's exceptional effectiveness:

> The industrial setting and . . . the best elements of institutional and on-the-job training, . . .
>> Instructors are craftsmen, with current industrial experience
>> A painstaking recruitment/selection process
>> Shop training is rigorous, relatively lengthy, and individualized
>> Trade-related academic and remedial education
>> Close relationships with employers whose skill needs are known; a large placement network of satisfied employers
>> Comprehensive supportive services
>> Indepth union and community support
>> Strong management and program development services.

In 1972, a TAT advisory committee worked out a replication model, but the members found it hard to agree on which elements were crucial for success. Robert Schrank, a Ford Foundation manpower expert, felt it was "the live, apprentice nature of the training, with trainees under the wing of a journeyman who takes a personal interest. It may also be self-selection, with TAT attracting the best of the group."

For Allen Janger, of the Conference Board, the partnership between one company, Union Carbide, and an educational institution was the crucial ingredient. In the case of TAT, it is Oak Ridge Associated Universities (ORAU), which handles administration, research, and community relations. According to Janger, "This relationship provided stability, and from that came strong management."

Jack Fritts agrees about the importance of ORAU: It manages the placement system; it brings in company interviewers and gets feedback from them that it uses to modify the program; it helps graduates relocate (one-quarter take jobs through the Southeast); it organizes "industrial behavior" seminars, evaluates the graduates' experience, and handles trainees' problems; and it responds to the local sponsors that pay for the training.

"We have continuously advocated this program and looked for new funding," says Gary de Mik, head of research and development for ORAU. "Our tolerance for frustration is high because our staff is so closely connected to this work. We have an ongoing, self-interested commitment."

How They Fared

In 1972, ORAU surveyed 472 people who had successfully completed the TAT program. The findings are instructive.

Immediately after graduation, practically all the trainees moved into jobs at starting salaries close to the national average for production workers. About one-third were employed in local Union Carbide plants. More than sixty other employers had hired the other two-thirds, placing them in over 170 different jobs. Overall, TAT trainees had worked 90 percent of the time since graduation. Their unemployment rate was 9 percent, which was low for young workers. By comparison, only 37 percent of the enrollees had been employed before training.

For the class of 1972, the average annual income after training was $7,509. For those who had been employed before they entered the program, the average income was $4,484. The wage gain for the group was $3,025. For the class of 1969, the average income was $6,302; trainees in other government programs earned an average of $3,400. Thus, for 1969 TAT graduates, the average wage gain was $2,900; for graduates of other government programs, the average gain was $1,876.

The majority of graduates reported satisfaction with almost all aspects of their work, including pay, the company, co-workers, unions, supervisors, and the job as a whole. TAT graduates worked toward a better standard of living by moving to better housing, managing money responsibly, and striving for greater job competence. Furthermore, the TAT graduates were more active in community life than a control group was.

Most employers (87 percent) rated the performance of TAT graduates "adequate" to "superior."

In 1972, the cost for six months of training was $3,200 per trainee. That was somewhat lower than the cost per trainee (including completion of training and job placement) in other government-funded programs. Tuition in 1972 was $1,836 per trainee. At present, tuition is $2,640 per trainee (paid by CETA prime sponsors). The amounts of the subsistence and travel allowances vary depending on the sponsor, but in general, they are based on the minimum wage. They total about $2,400. Currently, total costs per TAT trainee are about $5,040.

A cost-benefit analysis showed that with the large wage gain, the rate of return to the individual was more than 200 percent. The analysis also showed that when both costs and taxes paid were taken into consideration, the rate of return to the federal government was 21 to 26 percent.

ALCOA

Summer Jobs for Youth

Since 1973, Alcoa's summer co-op program has increasingly focused on the training and personal development of women and members of minority groups for careers in engineering and business. The company makes a special effort to attract people from disadvantaged backgrounds because they constitute a largely untapped pool of talent. "We don't want to transfer into engineering and business only those young people who would otherwise go into law and medicine," explains Don Edwards, Alcoa's administrator for professional employment. "The greatest need is to increase the number of women and minorities who enter and stay in engineering schools."

During the summer of 1977, 101 young people worked at Alcoa's operating locations, laboratories, or sales offices for approximately three months. These students were placed in jobs that would acquaint them with the career opportunities available in business and industry. They assisted engineers, collected data, or contributed to a project. Most were college juniors and seniors enrolled in engineering programs, but high school and graduate students also participated. About three-fourths of the students were women and members of minority groups.

The largest number of minority and female participants come from schools with active programs directed to those groups and supported by the Alcoa Foundation. Summer employment at Alcoa thus provides many participants with additional financial support as well as vital work experience. Campus interviews are held to recruit students directly or to meet those who have already been recommended by co-op and education placement directors, deans of engineering, and faculty members.

Although the company does not judge the effectiveness of the program by the number of participants who later become employees, it does encourage those students who perform well to consider Alcoa for future employment. "The company has evaluated the summer program and has found the results to be extremely positive," says Edwards. "We insist that job assignments be meaningful. We believe that is an outstanding feature of the program. However, for that very reason, we might not be able to expand the number of students participating in the summer of 1978."

CONTINENTAL ILLINOIS NATIONAL BANK AND TRUST COMPANY

Work-Study Program Benefits both Young People and the Company

Since 1972, the Continental Illinois National Bank and Trust Company of Chicago has employed about 500 youths in a half-time split between school and work. These work-study employees range in age from 16 to 21. In 1977, Continental hired 140 students and was one of the city's largest work-study employers in the office occupations category.

The bank has just completed an evaluation of its work-study experience. It compared these young permanent part-time employees with two groups of regular hires (employees in the same age-group and employees in the same salary grades) that included both full-time and part-time employees. The results are very positive. Work-study employees had a higher job-retention rate, were rated somewhat superior in job performance, and had a better attendance record. Furthermore, those cooperative education students who later joined the bank as full-time employees cost the company somewhat less per hire than off-the-street hires.

Owen C. Johnson, vice president of personnel, says the bank has concluded that the program has been good for all concerned. "The employees gain a much better knowledge of our company's methods and working environment and also a much clearer idea of what kinds of full-time jobs to aim for. The system also benefits the company by enabling it to take a close look at cooperative education employees *before* they are hired full time."

Brenda Russell, coordinator of Continental Bank's program, states that the work-study arrangement "allows business to share in the development of the student. These youths become better performers when they shift to full-time work because they don't have the adjustment problems experienced by young regular hires. They have a remarkably better absentee rate, and while they are here, they perform better. So we win all three ways."

Kery McIntosh, a 17-year-old high school senior who works half time at Continental as a typist, says, "I am a step ahead in seeing if I like the business world. Sometimes, I feel older than the kids at school. I work in personnel here and am thinking of going to college to train in personnel work."

Rick Simonton, another 17-year-old senior in the personnel department, is equally enthusiastic. "Work attitudes are most important—like not turning down any new assignment and feeling that you can do the job. I think I am more mature now. Other kids with regular part-time jobs can call in sick and not be missed. Here, you have some responsibility. If you stay out, the work won't get done, and it will set everyone back."

Owen Johnson feels that there are not nearly enough work-study programs for high school and college students. He asserts that the number of cooperative education programs might be expanded considerably if employers would hire more part-time workers and if school systems would give higher priority to such programs. Johnson believes that the schools must become more flexible organizationally if this need is to be met.

About 9,000 Chicago public school students take part in a variety of cooperative education programs; however, they constitute only about 2 percent of all eligible students. Continental Bank is employing 140 students this year and is thus one of the largest employers of those in the office occupations category of work-study programs. Johnson and other personnel managers are urging the Chicago Board of Education to promote more flexible class schedules. The aim is to enable more students to work in the morning and go to school in the afternoon. For example, over 90 percent of the high school students employed at Continental come to work after morning classes. If a second shift of students could be developed, two students could share one full-time job, and more students could be hired.

EASTMAN KODAK COMPANY

Teens on Patrol

The summer of 1977 marked the eleventh year for Teens on Patrol (TOP), a program developed by Eastman Kodak in cooperation with the Rochester, New York, police force. TOP has given responsible roles to 1,042 young people, who patrol city recreation areas popular with youths, perform clerical chores at police headquarters, or regularly accompany police officers in patrol cars on calls for police assistance. The teen-agers are paid the minimum wage for a five-hour working day. TOP is very popular. More than 800 youths between the ages of 16 and 19 applied in 1977 for approximately 100 openings.

Each summer, Kodak grants about $100,000 to Rochester Jobs Inc. (RJI), an employment consortium of business, religious, and community agency leaders, to administer TOP. According to Kenneth Howard of Kodak's Personnel Relations Department, the teen-age participants in TOP have exerted a positive influence on their peers. In addition, their work with TOP has given these youths a good understanding of the police role and a sense of responsibility and dependability.

Captain Charles Price, who heads the police department's Community Services Unit, says, "We look at TOP, not as a training ground for future policemen, but as an opportunity for youngsters to find out the role of the police officer by working side by side with him."

A second major program inspired and funded by Kodak is the World of Work (WOW). WOW was launched in 1970 with a Kodak grant of $75,000 and the commitment of Kodak personnel as instructors. In its first year, some twenty-five high school students participated in this work-study program. WOW subsequently received a two-year grant from the Labor Department, and enrollment increased to 100. Enrollment continues to grow; in the school year 1977–78, 230 students will participate.

Today, the program is administered by RJI in cooperation with the Rochester city school district and the Board of Cooperative Educational Services for schools in eastern Monroe County. The program integrates work and education for students who have dropped out of high school or who are seriously considering dropping out. WOW students are taught skilled trades, such as carpentry, plumbing, electricity, and painting, while carrying out building renovations for Rochester-area nonprofit agencies or city housing agencies. They work a maximum of twenty-four hours per week at the minimum wage. They also carry a normal course load and attend five hours of classes on the days they are not working. RJI estimates that as a result of the program, about 50 percent of the participants have earned a high school diploma or its equivalent. Moreover, some 100 WOW graduates are now on the Kodak payroll.

Kodak has granted $1 million to RJI in the past ten years for these two programs alone. The primary goals, Kodak says, are to improve job preparation for the young and the disadvantaged and to improve the quality of life in the community. There is also a secondary goal: to produce good job prospects for the company.

EMORY UNIVERSITY

Flexible Career and Work Experience

Emory University in Atlanta, Georgia, encourages its students to explore career possibilities through the Developing Interest in Career Experience (DICE) program. DICE, which was established in 1976, was initially supported by a grant from the Alcoa Foundation and is sponsored by the Emory Board of Visitors and the university's Career Planning and Placement Center. Since its inception, 100 students have participated in the program.

DICE enables students to learn about career alternatives while they are studying for their degrees, rather than after graduation. They participate in work relationships in Atlanta-area businesses and professional firms. DICE students test (and often confirm) their initial career interests by choosing from four available options: Through *career coaching*, students receive direct counseling about careers and occupations available with the host companies. An *externship* gives the student look-over-the-shoulder work experience in a host organization. Students work for three to five hours a week for several weeks without pay, observing and learning about the work tasks and responsibilities. An *internship* provides a defined period of paid employment with a host company. The conditions and type of work are decided by the host and the student. *Full-time summer employment* provides more extensive paid employment experience with a host organization. Students who choose this option receive preliminary career counseling from DICE personnel.

84

Emory believes that the traditional collegial system discourages meaningful interaction between academic and work experience and that the professional work force has too little input into the educational process. DICE makes this vital cross-fertilization possible.

The program also serves to strengthen the relationship between Emory and the business and professional people who serve as hosts to the students. In essence, the hosts are sharing an educational relationship with the university by enabling college students to learn more about the American free enterprise system. DICE also makes it possible for employers to take an in-depth look at potential employees while they are still students, without incurring any obligations or expensive commitments.

DICE students are routinely asked for their comments on the program. Their evaluations have been highly favorable. Here are some representative responses:

Sophomore: "I think this is an excellent program. I was dealt with in a very personal way that helped me see what my interests were and what careers I could pursue. I have recommended this program to my friends."

Junior: "I am going to work in my family business, perhaps taking two years off to pursue an MBA. The DICE experience has helped my perception of the business world outside the family business."

Senior: "Right now my career plans are very uncertain. There are many areas of business I am considering, and I'll have to wait and see what happens. The program let me explore the financial investment field very carefully, and in this regard, it was an excellent experience."

Recent graduate: "I now work at a public televison station in Texas. I feel that my internship had a great deal to do with the fact that I got a job here. Just that little bit of experience goes a long way. People feel a lot better about hiring someone who has worked, even if only for a short time, in the area in which they are applying for a job. Working at the station in Atlanta gave me some contacts here in Texas, so I was able to go directly to the right person when I applied. It was probably the most practical course I could have taken at Emory."

In 1974, the Department of Health, Education, and Welfare's Task Force on Work in America concluded that "education is more meaningful if it has a work component; work is more meaningful if it has components of education and leisure."* DICE makes this conclusion a reality.

---

*James O'Toole, "Regional Spotlight," *Southern Regional Educational Board* 9, no. 2 (November 1974).

GENERAL ELECTRIC COMPANY

A Variety of Career Education Programs

Despite the persistent shortages of skilled craftsmen and technicians, America's colleges continue to graduate large numbers of majors in education, the humanities, and the social sciences. General Electric recognized this trend more than twenty years ago and has been actively engaged in efforts to reverse it. The company believes that the best way to reduce high unemployment among teen-agers and young adults and at the same time relieve the shortages of personnel in industrial occupations is to educate the educators. Joseph M. Bertotti, GE's manager of corporate educational relations, recently observed that "most educators have little knowledge of, or experience in, industrial occupations. They need opportunities to attend seminars that will give them a firsthand awareness of the industrial workplace."

Summer Fellowship Programs

Since 1959, GE has conducted the Career Education and Guidance Programs. These summer institutes began at Syracuse University and have expanded over the years to Boston University and the Universities of Louisville, South Carolina, and Indiana. These universities receive grants from GE to cover room, board, and tuition expenses for each participating secondary school teacher. Graduate credits are earned by those who complete the six-week program. About 2,000 persons have attended the institutes since the program's inception.

The summer program is designed to provide essential firsthand experience in industry for thousands of secondary school teachers and counselors. There are formal training courses structured and conducted by university faculty members. In addition, teachers and counselors shadow assigned employees in GE plants and other industries. They learn technical skills, work practices, and wage scales; and they observe employee attitudes, behavior, and motivations. Initially, one teacher shadowed one employee, but the concept of team shadowing (involving five teachers) developed when it became apparent that the team effort stimulated discussions and prompted the teachers to initiate innovative career programs in their schools.

Bertotti emphasizes the fact that "the summer institutes provide industrial career *education*, not simply career guidance information." Exposure to plant work increases the educators' awareness of the occupational opportunities available in industry and improves their ability to counsel young people about career choices. This, in turn, can ease the transition of youths from school to work.

In-Service Programs for Educators

The concept of team shadowing led to the development of the in-service Educator-in-Industry activities. The pioneer project began in Louisville, Kentucky, and Lynn, Massachusetts, where GE had long-standing relationships with both the secondary school systems and the local universities. These relationships enabled GE to build upon ideas generated at the summer institutes. The Educator-in-Industry concept has spread to other GE plant communities. Programs have been established or are anticipated in Erie, Pennsylvania; Portsmouth, Virginia; Bloomington, Indiana; San Jose, California; Schenectady and Syracuse, New York; Cincinnati and Cleveland, Ohio; and Bridgeport, Connecticut.

The programs, which are conducted during the school year, are open to teams of secondary school teachers, counselors, and administrators. Those who complete the programs, which last for twelve to fifteen weeks, earn graduate credits, and additional credits are offered for follow-up projects. The programs are planned and implemented by local college faculties in cooperation with representatives from local industries. The workshops, which are held after school hours at participating local colleges or industries, explore topics of specific interest to participants. Subjects vary from city to city, depending upon the local employment market. Workshops are supplemented by in-plant visits during which participants spend a full day shadowing assigned employees. Graduates of the program are unanimous in their endorsement of the shadow concept.

GE Community Programs for Young People

A large number of people are needed by General Electric to make and sell its products. They represent a wide variety of education, training, and experience. The continuing need for these people and the belief that career education plays a critical role in developing the human resources necessary for maintaining a strong economy have led to GE's commitment to career programs for young people.

The Program to Increase Minority Engineering Graduates (PIMEG) is GE's major career guidance program. It was initiated in 1973 and has become a part of the national effort, under the aegis of the National Academy of Engineering, to bring minority students into the field. The need for such an effort became obvious after analyses of engineering college enrollments showed that there were not enough minority engineering graduates to meet the hiring demands of high-technology companies. Today, there are well over 100 PIMEG programs in forty-nine plant communities.

PIMEG's activities center on a traveling exhibit called EXPO-TECH, which reaches minority students at the junior high or middle school level. It has five objectives: to inform students and interest them in engineering *before* they make critical course selections, to demonstrate the need to study mathematics and science in high school, to enlist support from teachers and counselors, to stimulate follow-up programs, and to create a national awareness of the need for minorities in engineering.

An EXPO-TECH trailer, which is equipped with exhibits ranging from simple machines to electronic devices, is designed to appeal to junior high and middle school students. The young people and their teachers tour the exhibit and handle the apparatus. It also features the Opportunity Theatre, a brief multimedia presentation about career opportunities in the world of engineering. Career information booklets are distributed, suggestions for follow-up classroom projects are offered, and ongoing activities involving local representatives of industry, minority associations, technical societies, and engineering colleges are encouraged.

Many cities visited by EXPO-TECH develop a long-range follow-up program to assure continuing guidance and assistance for students who want to pursue studies in engineering. In Philadelphia, the follow-up program led to the formation of Philadelphia Regional Introduction for Minorities in Engineering, Inc. (PRIME, Inc.). This tax-exempt nonprofit organization follows students through junior and senior high school and has increased the minority enrollment in Philadelphia's engineering colleges ninefold.

General Electric believes there is a need to tie publicity about career education to student interests. To this end, it has developed the multifaceted World-of-Work communications program, which is aimed at secondary school students. The program stimulates interest in the world of work through advertisements that relate work to student interests. The ads appear in monthly magazines, such as Scholastic Series and the Xerox Educational Publications, that are distributed to classrooms. They relate hobbies and everyday interests to career aptitudes, emphasize the importance of education in developing a natural talent, and attempt to break down traditional stereotypes. Readers are encouraged to talk with teachers and counselors about career possibilities and to write to General Electric for additional job-oriented booklets.

The program's staff responds immediately to requests for career booklets. *What's it Like to be a Technician* is a typical title. The booklets average twenty-four pages in length and contain colorful photographs of the world of work. Booklets are updated, and new series are prepared periodically.

World-of-Work enlists the participation of counselors and teachers in its communications programs. Teachers and counselors receive poster-size versions of the ads, and GE community-relations personnel participate in career days at the schools. GE also participates in the annual convention of the American Personnel and Guidance Association, where ads, posters, and booklets are available at the exhibit booth. Ideas engendered by discussions, comments, and suggestions stimulated by the exhibit are reflected in future ads and booklets.

In recent years, the World-of-Work program has been endorsed by the U.S. Office of Education's director of career education, various state education departments, the Department of Labor, and many educational and youth associations.

During the past few years, many GE plants and offices have become involved in other career education activities designed primarily for students: San Jose's In-Step Program offers high school accredited courses in engineering and science, after hours, at GE plant facilities. In Philadelphia, the Early Bird Program offers one-to-one tutoring in mathematics and science. National Alliance of Businessmen youth programs, Junior Achievement chapters, and Exploring Posts receive support from GE plants in Schenectady, Cleveland, and other cities.

KOPPERS COMPANY

Linking Employees and Students in a Cooperative Program

In 1974, Koppers Company, Inc., decided to centralize its cooperative education efforts in order to offer more relevant work experience to college students. The company's Human Resources Department expanded the number of work-study jobs, sending students to smaller company locations that had not previously participated in the program. The summer jobs program for college students has also been enlarged. Each Koppers location now recruits summer employees according to its own needs. However, salary rates and on-campus screening of candidates remain centrally coordinated.

Koppers, a diversified manufacturing company in the engineering and construction fields, finds that its school-to-work efforts are having an unexpected beneficial effect: They aid the development of those regular employees who work with and supervise the students. According to Fletcher L. Byrom, chairman of Koppers, "With a co-op student assigned to them for a work period, the employee must not only adhere to personal work schedules but must also learn to delegate responsibility without losing sight of the fact that he or she remains accountable for the *student's* results."

Other Programs for Youths

Koppers also participates in youth programs run by other organizations. These include Pittsburgh's Urban Youth Action, in which inner-city minority youths are offered part-time work experience and seminars on the industrial work environment; NAB's Guided Opportunities for Life Decisions (GOLD) work-experience program; and Junior Achievement's Project Business, in which company representatives team-teach a curriculum of business subjects and economic principles in local junior high schools.

Kopper's most interesting joint training effort for youths has been a program of teaching machine shop techniques to new high school graduates in the Baltimore area. The project is supported by Koppers and the state of Maryland. Three groups totaling forty-six people were trained during 1975. There were also smaller pilot programs for students interested in hydraulics and electronics. State authorities, although pleased with the results, have not yet followed up on these initial ventures.

Better Use of the State Employment Service

Koppers and a number of companies have joined with Pennsylvania's Bureau of Employment Security to improve job placements. State Employment Service counselors have been assigned to learn more about

Kopper's occupational needs so that they can respond quickly and effectively in referring qualified job candidates. The same interviewer now screens all individuals being considered for referral to the company.

MAYOR'S SUMMER PROGRAM FOR THE EMPLOYMENT OF DISADVANTAGED YOUTH

Nation's Largest Summer Jobs Program Is in Chicago

Chicago's Mayor's Summer Program for the Employment of Disadvantaged Youth (MSPEDY) is the largest program of its kind in the country. Together, the public sector and private nonprofit agencies employ about 46,000 youths between the ages of 14 and 21; the private sector hires 39,000 young people between the ages of 16 and 21. Chicagoans assert that no other city provides summer youth employment in either the public or private sector on the scale that Chicago does. New York, they note, offers about 30,000 public-sector summer jobs.

Since 1969, many Chicago public and private summer jobs programs for youth have been administered through the office of the mayor. In the program's first year, Commonwealth Edison provided the leadership for the private, profit-making sector. Today, there is a division for each industry. The chairman of each division, who is invariably the chief executive officer of a large company, conducts a city-wide campaign writing to other chief executives to ask for a report on the extent of their hiring of young people for summer jobs and to solicit their help.

This industry-by-industry approach has proved very productive. The metals and machines industry division, for example, has organized summer jobs programs in thirty companies.

Business and the Private Agencies

About half of the $24.7 million budget for summer jobs in the nonprofit sector was allocated to city agencies and half to private nonprofit agencies. The profit-making sector plays an important role here, too. Businessmen make significant contributions of time and effort to the private social agencies. Often, they provide financial assistance as well.

For example, George Yoxall, manager of personnel and training at Inland Steel Company, is past president of the Chicago Federation of Settlements, which in 1976 placed and supervised more than 1,700 young people in summer jobs. The jobs last for nine weeks, twenty-six hours a week. In 1975, participants earned $491 (at $2.10 per hour); in 1976, they earned $538 (at $2.30 per hour).

The federation, which is the largest single network of private social services in the city, is made up of eighty-one neighborhood-based settlements located throughout Chicago's inner city. It supervises over $3 million in federally supported programs for impoverished families.

"Most of the boards of Chicago's private agencies are made up of people from business," Yoxall says, "especially top company leaders. This is a tradition in our city."

Who Are MSPEDY's Clients?

Most of the students who benefit from MSPEDY's 85,000 summer jobs are disadvantaged. About five-eighths are members of minority groups. Minorities represent about 35 percent of Chicago's population. For the private sector as a whole, over 30 percent of the young people who participate in the summer jobs program are minorities. In the metals industry, 28 percent of the summer youth hires are minorities.

Whereas no income test is applied to applicants for summer jobs in the profit-making sector, all applicants for summer jobs with either city or private agencies must meet federal poverty guidelines. In the summer of 1975, the Federation of Settlements surveyed all 1,600 youths it was employing; 967 responded. A computer analysis of these responses provided the following profile of the federation's young summer employees: Average family size was 6.5 people. Average family income was $7,000. The majority (90 percent) of the youths were minorities, including 61 percent blacks, 27 percent Hispanics, and 2 percent Orientals. More than half (59 percent) were female. Thirty-seven percent lived in public housing, and 38 percent lived in overcrowded households (defined as more than two people per bedroom). Only 26 percent of these young employees reported that their household contained both parents. In 53 percent of the cases, the father was absent; in 12 percent, the mother was absent. Nine percent reported that neither their mother nor their father lived with them.

In 54 percent of these households, one or more persons were receiving public aid. The overall unemployment rate in the households of the 967 respondents was 21 percent. In 42 percent of the households, at least one person was unemployed and actively seeking work. At least one person was receiving an unemployment check in only 10 percent of respondents' households. At least one person was working full time in 54 percent of the households. And in 38 percent of the households, at least one person was receiving public aid, and one or more persons worked full time.

Respondents' households contained a total of 3,326 persons 16 years old or older. Of these, 64 percent were in the labor force (i.e., either employed or actively seeking employment). Respondents reported that 25.4 percent were working full time and that 25.6 percent were working part time. A total of 9.5 percent were actively seeking work, and 3.5 percent were receiving unemployment compensation.

In 1976, the Mayor's Office of Manpower (MOM) adapted the 1975 survey used by the Chicago Federation of Settlements and made a similar evaluation of the public-sector effort. It administered the survey to a random sample of 5,000 summer employees and received 3,460 usable returns (a response rate of 69 percent). MOM's monitoring staff was thorough. It also visited each of the 1,894 work sites an average of 3.3 times during the nine-week employment period.

The profile of this group of summer workers was in many ways similar to that of the group surveyed by the federation in 1975. Virtually all these youths met the poverty guidelines. One difference was that the age range dropped for 1976 to include 14-year-olds. Consequently, MOM found that 25 percent of its enrollees were 14 and 15 and that 75 percent were 16 to 21. This met the program's goal. However, only 1 percent of the participants were handicapped; whereas MSPEDY's goal was to enroll 3 to 5 percent handicapped young people. Over nine-tenths of these disadvantaged youths were members of minority groups (77 percent black and 16 percent Hispanic). For 20 percent of the participants, English was not the only language spoken at home. Women again outnumbered men (54 to 46 percent, respectively). Ninety percent were full-time students. Of these, 65 percent had a ninth to eleventh grade education, 15 percent were at or below the eighth grade level, 13 percent had reached the twelfth grade, and almost 7 percent had gone beyond high school.

Perhaps the most significant finding of MOM's evaluators was that "recruitment efforts for the summer program reached most community areas in proportion to their need."

The staff of the Illinois Bureau of Employment Security who reviewed MOM's paper work (a periodic audit) to see that it was in order found that "less than 1 percent of the enrollees were of questionable eligibility."

What the Youths Thought

Did MSPEDY achieve its goals of providing productive work and good learning experience? The MOM evaluators thought that it had. In their 1976 report, they noted:

> The results from the summer survey indicate that most summer participants had valuable, productive work experiences. Three-fourths felt that their summer experience was "good" or "very good." 54 percent said their summer job provided "good job training" and over 55 percent said that they "liked" their job. Additionally, 44 percent felt that their jobs were "interesting" and 31 percent said that they "had fun."

> A small percentage expressed some dissatisfaction: 8 percent indicated that there was "not enough work" and 5 percent stated that their job was "boring." 6 percent said that they "worked too hard" and that they "did not like" their jobs. Only 2 percent felt that their program experience was generally "bad."

> The results of the survey also indicated that the summer program provides real and useful work experiences, as well as teaching valuable skills. 57 percent of the participants stated that they "learned to work with people," and 30 percent stated that they "learned to deal with a boss." Additionally, 43 percent felt that they "learned some skills that might help them get jobs." 9 percent stated that they "changed the way [they] felt about school."

> The participants also indicated that the money earned during the summer was extremely useful. 60 percent stated that they "earned needed money." However, all enrollees stated home or school-related uses of their summer income. 52 percent stated that they would use their summer income for school costs. The remaining 48 percent would use the money for: 1) parents and family, 2) themselves, 3) savings, and 4) their expected or existing offspring.

One major conclusion of the MOM evaluation was that

> Good supervision is the most important ingredient in providing a valuable and realistic work experience. Where supervision is firm, fair and consistent, summer jobs provide good experience, even in situations where job activities are routine.

> Questionnaire results strongly confirm this conclusion. The aggregate supervisor ratings were strongly positive. Almost one-third of the participants rated their supervisor "excellent" and 62 percent rated them "O.K." . . . Supervision is very highly correlated with program quality.

Useful Jobs

Another highly significant finding of the MOM evaluation was that the participants want jobs that provide them with both sufficient work and variety in the daily routine. What were the MSPEDY jobs? Their descriptions indicate that they are socially useful. The 1976 MOM evaluation offered the following report:

> Included were jobs as health aides, assistants to the blind, performers in music or drama groups, and office workers. Model Cities–CCUO youths painted murals and fire hydrants and worked in laboratories, hospitals, community organizations, and day care centers. Some rehabilitated housing, others cleared railroad embankments and cleaned underpasses.

> Through the Chicago Board of Education. . . . many tutored younger students. At the Archdiocese of Chicago School Board, enrollees not only worked at parochial grammar and high schools, but at child care centers and homes for the aged.

> Another agency, the YMCA, assigned enrollees to teach children arts and crafts, supervise games in playlots, pools and on basketball courts and in day camps. Youths with an interest in medicine got a chance to serve in medical laboratories and hospitals, assist in blood bank programs, or work with the blind or mentally retarded.

> Working for the Chicago Park District meant a job either as a landscape or recreation aide. . . . The Chicago Housing Authority hired residents of the

city's public housing projects. Work included gardening, community clean-up, and tutoring children.

Through the City Colleges of Chicago, enrollees spent two hours daily studying English and mathematics, and three hours working throughout schools as recreation and clerical aids, landscaping school grounds, helping out in lunchrooms and school buildings.

These jobs, the MOM evaluators concluded, lead to "meaningful work experiences in which [the young participants] often learn skills and develop attitudes that increase their chances for future success in employment."

MEAD CORPORATION

Developing Skills in Young Employees and Co-Op Students

The Mead Corporation, a natural resources company producing forest, paper, and paperboard products, has its headquarters in Dayton, Ohio. A domestic work force of 27,300 is employed at 140 company locations. In some locations, particularly in the Southeast, over 50 percent of new employees are minority individuals. In all areas, Mead's hiring policies are aimed at reflecting local worker-availability patterns.

Because about 1,600 (80 percent) of the 2,000 people hired annually are inexperienced and many of them are young, Mead offers a broad range of OJT programs. Those receiving training are generally new to the work force as well as to Mead.

The training program varies according to the job assignment and the individual's skills and talents. Training in manual skills tends to be fairly routine and can be completed within a short time. The development of salaried employees is more individualized, and training is generally provided through periodic workshops or seminars. At the management level, about 250 employees attend the Mead Management Institute each year. Its programs are geared to upgrading those who are already managers and to developing those professionals who have the potential for leadership. The traveling faculty of this institute without walls teaches three distinct curricula: orientation, functional skills, and management skills. Mead also offers opportunities for employee self-development through a program of partial tuition assistance. Vietnam-era veterans frequently receive government assistance as well, so that their educational expenses are covered in full.

Mead also offers programs aimed at recruiting and training special-potential employee groups. For example, the three-year-old Engineering Co-op attracts twelve engineering college students each year; most are specializing in mechanical or civil engineering. Students work full time at Mead pulp and paper mills for three months, spend the next three months on campus, and then return to Mead for new assignments. They begin their co-op program working at tasks commensurate with their backgrounds. As they progress through their college work, their field assignments at Mead become increasingly challenging.

Managers at the company's Mulga Mine near Birmingham, Alabama, are actively involved in the mining curriculum of Walker Technical School as guest lecturers on mine safety engineering. The company hopes to stimulate interest in mining by familiarizing the students with actual mining practices and problems. Employees at the mine are encouraged to register for the Walker program through Mead's tuition assistance plan.

NORTHWESTERN MUTUAL LIFE INSURANCE COMPANY

Providing Training and Greater Job Opportunities

Northwestern Mutual hires an average of 350 people each year. More than 50 percent of these new employees are 20 years of age or younger. The company has thus gained considerable experience in school-to-work and youth training programs.

For sixteen years, Northwestern has taken part in a cooperative education project for Milwaukee high school students. From twenty to twenty-five teen-agers work at the company for half a day and go to school the other half day. Northwestern Mutual emphasizes that these jobs meet the need for extra help in various departments, that they are not simply make-work spots. "The program is productive for us *and* for the students," says James Ehrenstrom, manager of industrial relations. "About 98 percent of these young people return to the company for full-time or part-time work after they graduate."

In recent years, the company has tried a number of approaches to training the hard-to-employ and has concluded that on-the-job training is the most effective. Accordingly, close to 10 percent of new employees (twenty-five to thirty-five people) are hired for entry-level OJT positions each year. Most of these trainees are members of minority groups and have below-average academic backgrounds and insufficient job skills. They are trained for clerical or semiprofessional positions and receive additional aid for further training through tuition refunds.

In 1973, Northwestern instituted variable hours, thus further widening the range of job opportunities it can offer, particularly to working mothers. Under the variable hours arrangement, employees select their starting time (between 7:00 and 9:00 A.M.) and leaving time (between 3:00 and 5:00 P.M.) and are required to maintain their chosen schedule.

The company is also slowly increasing the size of its part-time work force, and employee benefits have been extended to the part-timers.

In addition, Northwestern has instituted some job sharing over the last two years. At present, eight full-time positions, mostly entry-level clerical jobs, are shared by two people each. For example, eight to ten people share jobs involving mailing out insurance policies. Although job sharing at Northwestern is still limited, it has proved highly successful.

PACIFIC GAS & ELECTRIC COMPANY

Introducing Young People to the Workplace

About twenty employees of Pacific Gas and Electric (PG&E) receive one-half day's release time each week to tutor elementary and high school students in the San Francisco Bay Area. This program, which is three years old, has so far been limited to the company's main office because most employees in the field are construction workers. However, PG&E hopes to extend participation in the tutoring program to field employees within one or two years.

PG&E has also developed a program of tours of the company's offices for elementary and high school students. Its goal is to acquaint the students with the various types of careers that the company offers. Tours last a morning or an afternoon. After an orientation session, the students visit the design-drafting, customer service, and office services departments.

The project's principal aim is to provide career guidance. Although the company feels that it eventually receives job applications from students who have participated in the tour program, no direct link is traceable.

PG&E is also hoping to substantially increase the number of female and minority engineering students who are enrolled in a special long-term work-experience program of part-time or summer work with the company. Twenty students have participated in the engineering program since its inception in 1973.

PRUDENTIAL
INSURANCE COMPANY OF AMERICA

Special Education for Youths and Adults

Many large companies contribute to local education efforts, but the Prudential Insurance Company of America provides support for an unusually wide range of special-education programs. Its activities can be divided into two main groups: those that benefit disadvantaged youths and those that aid Prudential's employees or older people in the community.

Tutoring Programs

Project LINK, an alternative school in Newark (the location of Prudential's corporate headquarters), is designed for sixth, seventh, and eighth graders who have been unable to achieve in the normal school setting. Students are brought to Prudential weekly to participate in enrichment workshops conducted by a team of tutors. Subjects include drama, business, and foreign cultures. Over 100 LINK students participate in this program during the school year.

Prudential employees participate in a weekly one-to-one tutoring program in basic arithmetic and reading skills for thirty-five teen-agers from Newark's Montgomery Street School, a special facility for the handicapped. Many participants are mentally retarded individuals who are considered educable.

Prudential also runs an after-hours tutorial program that provides one-to-one remedial help in mathematics and reading and group counseling to thirty Hispanic teen-agers. Most of these students come from Juveniles in Need of Supervision (JINS), a remedial program run by Focus and La Casa de Don Pedro, two youth development centers in Newark.

Dinner in the company cafeteria is provided for both tutors and students participating in these three programs.

During the workday, Prudential employees travel to the Mount Vernon Elementary School where, each week, they provide individualized remedial tutoring in reading and arithmetic to about twenty students in the fourth to sixth grades. Although Mount Vernon's student population is 70 percent nonminority and has one of the highest achievement ratings in the city, the Prudential program aids students who come from non-English-speaking homes or who are bussed in from other districts and need remedial tutoring to reach grade level.

More than twenty Prudential employees participate in School Volunteers for Boston, another special-education program. They spend a half day each week during the school year at inner-city elementary schools, where they tutor, aid teachers, and in some cases, conduct classes. School Volunteers for Boston feels this program, which has been in existence for more than ten years, has proved highly successful.

Career Education–Work Partnerships

For thirteen years, Prudential has been one of the Newark companies providing work-study jobs for students from the Education Center for Youth, an alternative school for dropouts sponsored by the Newark Board of Education. Two students are assigned to one full-time Prudential job. While one student attends school full time for a week, the other is on the job at Prudential. They alternate on a weekly basis. After graduation, many of these students begin full-time employment with their sponsoring departments. Although the number of work-study jobs varies with department need, sixty students now share thirty jobs. Prudential feels that work-study participants who graduate into full-time jobs have a higher success rate than regular off-the-street hires. Graduates are already familiar with the company, have had more opportunity for counseling, and have acquired better skills while in the program.

Prudential has prepared a videotape on career orientation that is being used throughout the Newark senior high school system. The tape shows both wrong and right ways to approach a job interview and illustrates some of the problems that young people are likely to encounter after starting a job.

Both the JFK School and the Montgomery Street School are facilities for the trainable mentally retarded. Prudential raised $20,000 in a fundraising drive for the after-school recreation program at JFK. The company employs students from these schools part time while they are still in school and full time after they graduate. Prudential currently employs three students part time and three full time in the food service and maintenance areas.

For ten years, the company has offered summer jobs to students of Hampton Institute and permanent employment to its graduates. Hampton, a college with a predominantly black enrollment, is located in Hampton, Virginia.

University High, formerly known as School within a School (SWAS) because of its location within Malcolm X Shabazz High School, is a prestigious special school for college-bound Newark high school students. It offers college-preparatory courses at a level of instruction not available at other Newark schools and is in session eleven months of the year. It draws on the resources of several Newark-area colleges, including Rutgers State University and the New Jersey Institute of Technology. One of the special courses offered during the summer months is an actuarial mathematics course taught at Prudential by staff actuaries. In addition, when Prudential found that many of the school's graduates lacked funds for college, it established a scholarship fund and sought contributions from Newark businesses. Some University High graduates who have gone on to college are employed at Prudential in an NAB-sponsored summer jobs program. Recently, through funds made available by Prudential, University High moved into its own new building.

Ten years ago, the city of Boston established the School Partnership Program, in which large corporations work closely with inner-city high schools to help enrich curricula and offer career counseling and other vocational services. Prudential's partnership institution is Boston High School, a special facility for teen-agers who have dropped out of other high schools. Prudential has helped in a variety of ways, including the development of a school newspaper and yearbook and the organization of various extracurricular activities.

A number of minority students from Northeastern University in Boston have joined the company in intermediate-level technical and clerical work-study positions. Prudential pays 80 percent of their tuition.

Since 1974, six Prudential Scholars have been selected each year from Johnson C. Smith University, a predominantly black college in Charlotte, North Carolina. The company provides the funds for these students to take computer sciences courses at the college. There have been thirty scholarship winners so far, and several Prudential Scholars have already begun careers with the company.

Prudential employees participate in the Youth Motivation Task Force programs in Boston and Los Angeles. All the task force participants are members of minority groups. They conduct seminars at junior and senior high schools in which they emphasize the importance of staying in school and getting an education, pointing to their own careers as evidence that education can pay off.

Special Programs for Adults

College in the Company is a joint educational effort sponsored by Prudential's corporate headquarters and Essex County College, with Prudential serving as an extension center. The program offers many college credit and noncredit courses taught by Prudential employees at the company's facilities. Employees who serve as teachers are paid as adjuncts by the college. College in the Company is open to both current and retired Prudential employees, and students can earn degrees if they also attend classes at the college campus. Similar programs have been undertaken at Prudential's offices in Boston, Jacksonville, and South Plainfield.

The company offers a course in English as a second language for employees whose native tongue is not English and whose jobs require a better command of the language.

Prudential has established a temporary-work program that utilizes the talents of senior citizens. The company has direct contracts with local organizations to recruit qualified individuals for temporary clerical assignments. Thirty-one of these senior citizens are currently on the payroll as temporaries. Two have become permanent full-time employees. Participating community organizations include the North Ward Educational and Cultural Center, the Salvation Army Ironbound Boy's Club, and the Unified Vailsburg Services Organization.

RALSTON PURINA COMPANY

Summer Jobs Nationwide

Seven years ago, the Ralston Purina Company initiated a summer job program that now involves more than 500 high school juniors and seniors across the country. The company limits the program to inner-city or disadvantaged youths. Young people from the suburbs qualify if they are dependents of low-income families, and juvenile offenders are also eligible. Participants are employed by various social agencies and minority businesses for twenty hours each week. The employing organization and Ralston Purina agree on the work to be done, and Ralston Purina pays the youths' wages. In many cases, these summer jobs are their first paid work experience. In at least one case, the Institute of Black Studies in Saint Louis, the students receive additional help in applying to colleges and for scholarship aid.

To assure itself that the various programs are adequately supervised, Ralston Purina solicits nonprofit organizations nationwide to develop summer jobs, particularly among minority businesses. Although the program is not supported by any other organization, public or private, Ralston Purina provides information about the program to companies that request it.

On-Site Work-Study Program

In a separate activity, Ralston Purina participates in a work-study program organized by the Saint Louis public school system. Each year, approximately thirty-five high school seniors study in on-site classrooms during the morning and work at paid jobs with the company during the afternoon. The learning materials and the teachers are provided by the school system. The program, which was initiated in 1967, began with one teacher. It has been expanded to include two teachers, and the students are divided into two classes.

In any given year, twenty-five to thirty of the participating students stay on as Ralston Purina employees after graduation. Most of the other students enter college. The program has had few dropouts. In contrast, the company believes that without the alternative of the work-study program, many of these young people would have dropped out of high school.

R. L. Maxwell, director of organization development for Ralston Purina, says that the company feels confident in recommending the program to other companies. Maxwell reports that Ralston Purina has found the work-study students who complete the program to be much better prepared for the workplace than other inner-city youths interviewed or hired by the company.

TEXAS INSTRUMENTS

Engineering Development for Young Employees

Young employees who have the ability and desire to become engineers but who lack the money for schooling have been aided in an unusual program at Texas Instruments Incorporated in Dallas, Texas. It provides educational reimbursement for the time that its participants are in school; the amount of payments varies according to the individual's educational status and length of service with the company. Employees are given four hours off each day to attend classes at one of the several participating engineering schools; they also work four hours a day. The combination of work income and educational aid is sufficient to support the students while they attend engineering college.

In selecting participants, the company gives priority to employees and the children of employees; it then considers deserving youths from the surrounding community. The program currently includes more than 200 students, 80 percent of them Texas Instruments employees. Minority individuals are well represented.

The company points to several complementary benefits of the program: It provides an opportunity for an engineering education for employees and others who lack sufficient income for college, gives financial support to several educational institutions, and develops a source of engineering talent for the future.

3 TRAINING AND JOBS FOR THE UNEMPLOYED WITH SPECIAL DISADVANTAGES

BORG-WARNER CORPORATION

Training the Disadvantaged, Hiring Ex-Offenders, and Counseling Young People

The Borg-Warner Corporation in Chicago was one of hundreds of companies that signed up between 1968 and 1970 to train disadvantaged people through Job Opportunities in the Business Sector (JOBS). JOBS was established by the National Alliance of Businessmen (NAB) in response to urban needs, the prodding of President Lyndon B. Johnson, and a new awareness of the responsibility of American businessmen to help reduce unemployment among the disadvantaged.

Most participating companies scaled back their training and hiring efforts in the early 1970s, although they continued to take part in NAB job pledge and hiring compaigns. But Borg-Warner did not cut back on its program except during the most severe period of the 1974–75 recession. At that time, many Borg-Warner workers were on layoffs, and the company felt that it could not add new trainees until most workers were recalled. Consequently, the number of trainees was sharply reduced.

Borg-Warner's program has produced an average of fifty trainees annually since 1968; in 1977, the total was raised to ninety. Classes graduated in February, May, and September. The project started as Jobs-70, and was geared to training disadvantaged persons. (A disadvantaged person was defined as a member of a minority group or anyone who had been unemployed or on welfare for over twenty-one weeks.) At first, Borg-Warner had very few minority individuals in its plants; but today, members of minority groups constitute about 26 percent of the company's 3,800 employees in the Chicago area and 12 percent of its 26,000 employees nationwide.

Most training takes place on the job. It includes learning to operate machines or assemble parts and to cope with the demands of production work. A maximum of 100 hours of classroom training is included. The total training time varies according to the type of job; the Labor Department's *Dictionary of Occupational Titles* prescribes a standard number of training hours for each job. An assembler is trained in 550 hours, or three months; a machine operator needs 1,390 hours, or eight months. The classroom study is interspersed. For example, in many shops, eight hours of classes are given one day a week.

The training has been federally subsidized, first by Labor Department funds and since 1974 by CETA funds. The average cost to the government has been about $2,000 per trainee, which is less than the cost of most on-the-job training. The company pays the cost of four staff members (two teachers, a manager, and a counselor).

Borg-Warner conducts an annual evaluation of the program. "Our overall retention rate, counted at the end of each contract period, has been about 80 percent," says Kaye Ellis, manager of special employment. "Some divisions showed 100 percent retention; others, 75 percent. None was lower than 70 percent. It often has to do with working conditions; some locations show very different retention rates. However, the overall retention rate and performance of the trainees have been as good as those of the regular entry-level employees; in some cases, they have been better. One reason may be the counseling our trainees receive, which is not available to regular hires. Also, the trainees can continue to receive counseling as needed after they have completed their training."

Ellis explains that Borg-Warner does not plan to continue the Jobs-70 program in 1978 "because now we want to upgrade our minority and female employees and help them into high-level jobs. Furthermore, even unskilled disadvantaged and minority people can now get a factory job with us through normal channels and receive regular on-the-job training."

Youth Motivation and Career Education

The company has three programs that are designed to motivate youths to seek a higher education and to introduce them to the kinds of jobs found at Borg-Warner: Each year, local high schools recommend forty to fifty seniors for a one-day work experience in whatever department of the company each student chooses; high school seniors take tours through the company's various locations and also receive an orientation lecture in a classroom setting; and about 600 students attend career nights at local high schools at which company representatives tell the students about college course requirements for Borg-Warner jobs, starting salaries, and advancement opportunities, particularly for women. These activities are aimed at overcoming what the company feels is generally inadequate career information and counseling provided by the schools.

Hiring Ex-Offenders

Borg-Warner hired Richard H. Brown, an ex-offender, as its employee-relations coordinator. A skilled audio-video technician, Brown was responsible for the taping of the company's training programs as well as for coordinating training materials. In April 1977, he left to become a cameraman for NBC-TV in Chicago.

For the past two years, Borg-Warner has screened ex-offender applicants recommended for employment by the Safer Foundation and similar agencies in Chicago. To her knowledge, Ellis says, Borg-Warner has hired at least fifteen ex-offenders at its Chicago operations since 1975. However, because ex-offender status is confidential, and because the screening procedure is unique to the Chicago office, Borg-Warner's corporate office does not know how many have been hired by its divisions nationwide.

CHEMICAL BANK

Special Training Helped Dropouts to Achieve Good Job Records

In 1968 and 1969, Chemical Bank in New York participated in the local NAB JOBS effort, run by the New York Urban Coalition. Until about

1974, hundreds of companies participated in the coalition's JOBS consortia, with the companies making commitments for job slots and the Chamber subcontracting the training to professional training firms. From 1969 to 1974, over 1,500 people took part in training programs, each lasting sixteen to twenty weeks. The effort gradually collapsed for a variety of reasons, including a lapse in federal funds and a decline of the local NAB. In 1969, says Thomas Barile, Chemical Bank's head of special recruitment, "we decided that we could do a better job of training for ourselves, using our own staff." The result was the Jobs Program. It was initiated in June 1969 and continued until mid-1974. During that time, an average of 120 people were graduated from the program each year, for a total of about 800 graduates.

Participants had to be 16 to 22 years of age or over 45. Almost all were members of minority groups; 99 percent were black or Hispanic. "We were mostly training women," Barile says. "Our problem was to attract men. Our trainees were mostly young people, and of those, all were high school dropouts." All entrants had to have a "certification of poverty" based on family income. Referrals came to Chemical from the Manpower & Career Development Association, which is a city agency, and from the New York State Employment Service. "Although they ostensibly screened applicants," Barile says, "the job counselors in these organizations were rated on the number of people sent for job interviews, and quality didn't seem to matter. In fact, we had to establish who to take referrals from, which job counselors could fill our needs. In reality, some centers never really delivered."

When Barile took over management of the program in 1971, it was costing the bank about $500,000 annually, in addition to the $300,000 to $500,000 of federal funds it received. He reduced costs without reducing the number of trainees. Annual costs were cut to about $225,000 for the bank and $225,000 for the government, or just over $4,170 per trainee. This fifty-fifty split was considered desirable, but it was far from the original assertion by Coalition Jobs that this program would cost participating companies nothing. The greater part of the savings came from better screening of candidates and, above all, reduced turnover. Chemical Bank was reimbursed from $10 to $13 per person per day. The length of the training period was determined according to the government's *Dictionary of Occupational Titles*. The program employed a staff of thirteen professionals, and the facilities alone cost $120,000 per year.

"We got good people from the program," Barile says, "but sometimes we wondered if the benefits were worth the costs and the headaches. We had to negotiate *each* contract separately with the Department of Labor and without assurance of a follow-up contract. That meant we couldn't plan ahead. The bank felt that in these negotiations, *we* represented the client's interests."

Chemical Bank considers that the effort was successful. "We were retaining 65 to 70 percent of the trainees for nine to twelve months after they started in the program," Barile notes. "That was a very good proportion. The Labor Department considered six months' retention successful. It is hard to say what overall success is. At the time, our normal turnover in some categories, such as tellers, typists, and general entry-level positions, was 50 to 75 percent. Our trainees were bettering that considerably. In a 1972 study of the Operations Division, I found that our trainees were staying there six to eight months longer than the average off-the-street hires. In general, there are two peaks of turnover among our trainees: in the first three weeks of training and toward the end of the program cycle, when it was time for placement."

Problems with Bureaucracy

From 1969 to 1971, the length of time to get contract approval from the Labor Department was about twenty days. It rose to about sixty days in 1973, Barile notes. Then, when the new CETA law was passed in early 1974, the administration of the funds passed into local hands. At that point, Chemical Bank was in its fourteenth cycle of training contracts, and the bank tried through the New York Chamber of Commerce to find out what the new local mechanism for approving contracts would be. "We couldn't get a timetable for when a contract could be approved," Barile explains. "The city wasn't ready to administer contracts by June 1974. For every week without trainees, it would cost us $3,000 to maintain the staff and facilities. We had no choice but to phase out the program. The first CETA contract didn't come through until mid-1975, almost a year after we phased out. Even then, only seven private-sector contracts were given out. Locally, CETA didn't do very much with the private sector."

Barile states that the federal training program at that time suffered from excessive bureaucracy, which frustrated the private contractors, and also from a basic mistrust of the business community. Nevertheless, he believes that Chemical Bank's experience proves that "you can run a successful training program for the disadvantaged."

CHRYSLER INSTITUTE

Training as a Separate Business

The Entry-Level Training Department has made the Chrysler Institute, which is located in Center Line, Michigan, a leader in the hiring, training, and placing of the hard-core unemployed. Over the past ten years, the Chrysler Institute has served more than 50,000 disadvantaged clients. The institute was established in 1931 by Fred Zeder and Walter P. Chrysler. They realized that excellence in engineering is based on the excellence of employees, and so they invited the top engineering graduates in the country to the institute to participate in a two-year work-study program leading to a master's degree in automotive engineering. In the 1930s and 1940s, the institute offered evening classes for high school credits and diplomas. In the 1950s, classes in trade skills were given for those involved in apprenticeship programs; the purpose of these courses was to facilitate career advancement. In recent years, Chrysler Institute has joined with various colleges and universities to offer programs leading to bachelor's and master's degrees.

During the 1960s, the areas of Detroit that surround Chrysler Corporation became increasingly populated with disadvantaged and hard-to-employ persons. Chrysler sought ways to absorb these people, and at the same time, the Department of Labor, through the Manpower Development and Training Administration (MDTA), began to provide funds to encourage private business to hire, train, and retain the unemployed and disadvantaged. The Chrysler Institute responded to these challenges by developing, under MDTA, programs to prepare hard-to-employ and disadvantaged clients to move into the workplace. Chrysler Corporation thus became formally involved in hiring the disadvantaged. The institute launched the Entry-Level Training Department, which added objectives and responses in line with CETA requirements to its established entry-level program.

Chrysler Institute also began seeking jobs outside the automotive industry for clients who successfully completed training. A high percentage of these people have established successful careers. The institute attributes this rate of success to the realistic training experiences it provides. Employers who hire Chrysler Institute clients find them to be highly trained and well motivated, largely because of the multifaceted Entry-Level Training programs.

Comprehensive Programs

The Entry-Level Training Department also provides many government agencies with training and employment services as well as providing services for Chrysler's own needs. The Outreach and Recruitment program ensures an appropriate and equitable representation of disadvantaged people. The Assessment, Personal Career Plan, and Referral programs include testing and interviewing and help clients to obtain any necessary remedial training. One of the most dramatic programs in Entry-Level Training is Goal-Directed Group Counseling. It includes value classification, goal setting, and peer evaluation.

The Hands-on Training program is also an integral part of the Entry-Level Training Department. It allows the trainee-clients to learn and practice basic work skills in a simulated plant environment. The Skilled Training programs in welding, machining, power sewing, automotive repair, clerical skills, and other areas have been developed on the basis of a careful evaluation of the needs of the employment community.

The Job Survey and Development program identifies the needs and interests of the disadvantaged client in order to refer that client to the appropriate employer. Through Job Search, the clients themselves must actively seek employment. Clients are taught writing résumés and job applications, how to behave during a job interview, and how to retain a job. The institute may provide referrals, but clients are expected to do most of the job search work. When the institute places one of its clients with a company, the Placement and Follow-up program provides the assistance necessary to introduce the client to the new job and to assure his or her continuation in it. Both the Placement and Follow-up and the On-the-Job Training programs assist Chrysler supervisors in helping the new employee to become a successful part of the Chrysler work force.

The training programs developed and implemented by Chrysler Institute's Entry-Level Training Department have experienced impressive rates of success. Although the many program offerings vary substantially regarding clientele, content, and objectives, some general statistics can be offered. (These are generalizations from results of both the Detroit-area programs and the out-of-state operations. Currently, the institute is involved in programs in Saint Louis, Missouri; Cleveland, Toledo, and Lima, Ohio; Bogalusa, Louisiana; Brevard County, Florida; and elsewhere.) Approximately 80 percent of the clients finish the programs. Of those who complete the programs, nearly 75 percent are placed in nonsubsidized private-sector jobs that offer the potential for future growth.

However, placement alone is not the final objective. The staff of the Entry-Level Training Department is also concerned with the successful retention of the clients placed in jobs. It is therefore significant to note that almost 80 percent of the clients placed through Job Survey and Development are retained on their jobs and gain union seniority and job security.

Finally, there is the Staff Training program, which is one of the most critical services provided by Entry-Level Training. Through this program, Chrysler Institute people share their expertise in all areas with agencies, schools, and organizations that serve the same disadvantaged population.

CONTROL DATA CORPORATION

Providing Jobs in the Inner City

In January 1968, Control Data Corporation opened a new plant in the Northside community of Minneapolis. The company, which was expanding rapidly as a supplier of computer and financial services, had decided as a matter of social policy to create jobs in an area of high unemployment and low income. Control Data was confident that it could draw on its experience at several rural Midwestern plants to train unskilled people for jobs assembling electronic equipment.

The plant currently employs about 300 people, and the annual payroll is about $3.2 million. But the actual impact on the Northside community is much greater than the payroll alone indicates because this base of employment supports community merchants, contractors, and others who provide goods and services to the plant.

After consulting with community leaders, Control Data decided to select employees on a first-come, first-hired basis. Community agencies helped with recruiting among the unemployed, and application forms were reduced to one page. In its early years of operation, a large number of the employees hired were female heads of households. This was the first meaningful job for many of them — an important fact because these people often lacked a twelfth grade education. In addition, twenty high school graduates were trained as technicians; most of them are still with the company.

In the first three years of its operation, an estimated 770 people were trained and employed at the Northside plant. The cost was nearly $3,000 per job. Total extraordinary start-up costs were $2.3 million. The company paid $1.2 million, and the remaining $1.1 million came from a federal contract to train 270 of the new hires.

Within the first year of Northside's operation, Control Data made two critical decisions that greatly affected the success of the plant. The first was to give the Northside plant total responsibility for production of computer peripheral controllers and other assembly tasks. This meant that employment at Northside would be basically stable and that a wide range of job skills would be needed.

The second decision was to change Northside from a training facility to a profit-making center as quickly as possible. This meant that Northside employees were soon expected to improve their work performance to equal company-wide standards of efficiency and profitability. The Northside work force met the challenge of this change in work environment, becoming as productive as other Control Data employees. Frederick Green, manager of the Northside plant, states that the transition to a full emphasis on business and production criteria, rather than training, was essential to Northside's survival. "You can't run a plant as a training facility and then ask what profit it is making. Several inner-city plants in Minneapolis and a considerable number around the country closed for that reason between 1970 and 1972. We were told that we had to operate as efficiently as any plant in the company, and we have. Now we know that an individual's previous work record is not the main criterion in finding and developing a successful employee. If a person really wants to work, he or she can be trained to perform acceptably." Green feels that the surrounding Northside community has clearly benefited from the plant's profitability: "People here saw that we could be successful and changed their attitudes."

Those benefits include stable employment for residents, opportunities to move to higher-paying positions within the company, valuable work experience for those who have left, and greater confidence among residents that they can find employment. He points out that Control Data is constructing a large new facility in a depressed area of nearby Saint Paul, based in good part on the Northside experience. Green believes that more production facilities can be established in inner cities. However, he notes, that in many industries, technological change is resulting in a decreased labor input to production. For example, six to ten years ago, computer products contained a 40 percent labor input; today, they contain 7 percent. Consequently, technological innovation and capital investments are needed on a regular basis in order to maintain or expand production jobs. Moreover, because these jobs and their facilities are never entirely secure, a company that opens a new plant must deal with employees' fears that older plants may be closed.

"The key ingredient," Green feels, "is a company's commitment to stand by a new plant while it comes alive. That may take three or four years at the minimum. The company has to put in capable people and a stable product and insist on movement toward profitability. Government help can be important in terms of how much money a company is willing to lose in the early years, but government help won't make or break a plant."

CONTROL DATA CORPORATION

Providing Part-Time Work for Disadvantaged Mothers and Students at the Selby Bindery

Control Data's Selby Bindery is a unique industrial plant: It is structured on the concept of part-time employment. Selby employs 139 part-time workers. There is also a "backlog shift" of fifty-five people who are called in when the bindery is especially busy. (In addition, there are nine full-time staff members and supervisors.)

"We are the only part-time facility in the country, perhaps in the world," says Richard Mangram, manager of the bindery since its inception. "I don't know why there aren't other plants of this kind, but the part-time concept must grow because such work arrangements are so badly needed." Department of Labor figures support Mangram's opinion. They indicate that one-fifth of all unemployed persons are looking for part-time jobs only; twenty years ago, only one-tenth wanted part-time work.

The composition of Selby's work force is also unique: Seventy-five of the employees are women, most of them mothers with school-age children. Of the remaining regular employees, fifty-six are high school, college, or vocational school students who are working to put themselves through school or to supplement family income. Selby is thus fulfilling the purpose for which it was intended: to supply part-time employment primarily for female heads of households and mothers with school-age children and secondarily to neighborhood students. The concept originated with Norbert Berg, Control Data's senior vice president for administration and personnel.

The plant is located in the economically distressed Selby-Dale area of Saint Paul, Minnesota, a predominantly black neighborhood. At the start, in 1970, the bindery was housed in a renovated bowling alley; in 1974, it moved to larger quarters. Most of the employees (90 percent) are minority individuals. (By comparison, only 6.5 percent of the population of the surrounding city of Saint Paul is made up of members of minority groups.) Furthermore, most of the bindery's employees live in the neighborhood or the central city and are thus able to walk or take a bus to work. Selby is serving the people of its immediate neighborhood. Richard Mangram feels that this explains the "fierce loyalty" of the area's residents to the plant.

In its seven years of operation, Selby has been the training ground for about 150 employees who have gone on to higher-paying and higher-skilled full-time jobs. Twenty-four of these Selby workers were transferred to jobs at Control Data; the rest were placed with other employers. However, the total number of upgraded employees is even higher. Some people who applied for jobs at the bindery had good work records and were placed with other Twin Cities employers immediately.

Patricia Collins, who handles placement at Selby, emphasizes the work habits, experience, and references acquired by the employees. She believes that these factors may be the bindery's most useful contribution to the depressed Selby-Dale neighborhood, where unemployment is highest among minority women and teen-agers.

Efficiency

"Absenteeism is very low," Mangram says, "and we can always compensate by bringing in extra part-timers on any particular day. Furthermore, using part-time workers is efficient. No one can collate well for more than five hours at a time, which is all we schedule. Most people are less productive in their sixth to eighth hours of a workday. We are presumably getting the best five hours of our people's time."

Control Data Corporation has considerable evidence that the bindery is efficient. The Selby plant assembles tens of thousands of computer manuals and distributes them to Control Data customers all over the world. It also handles other corporations' mailings, such as shareholder reports and employee publications. In 1977, it expected to raise the proportion of its services sold to outside customers from 10 to 22 percent. Selby processes 7 million pieces of paper a month. Its total business volume is $500,000 a year, and in 1976, profits exceeded $20,000.

"Their charge was to save us money," says Norbert Berg. "Even now, they have to show me their costs regularly. Selby is a good business for us. We have economies of scale, a trained work force, and a good employee population."

Before the Selby facility was established, it cost Control Data nearly twice as much to have similar services performed by outside businesses. Today, Selby finds its costs are about half the charges of its competitors.

According to Mangram, low overhead, low absenteeism and turnover, and high productivity per worker account for Selby's competitiveness. "We have only two salespeople," he explains. "Our annual turnover has remained at 20 to 22 percent, which is quite low for part-time employees. Most leave for positive reasons, such as getting a full-time job. Only 3 percent a year leave and become unemployed. And we encourage our students who graduate from high school to find full-time jobs.

"Of course, the part-time arrangement won't work in every situation. Control Data considered part time an experiment for its first two years. Any company needs to give it time and may expect to lose money for a while if the work force is untrained."

Selby's size has been a factor in its success. In a small plant, managers can inform employees of the facility's income and costs on a monthly, weekly, or even daily basis and can get quick feedback on their performance. "We can identify any mistakes and correct them daily," Mangram explains. "We break down our costs for each job, and we tell them the results. This makes our people feel part of the institution."

Pay and Benefits

The average Selby employee earns $80 a week, or $320 a month. Of course, wages vary according to the job. For example, a binder-collator is paid $2.97 per hour; a binder helper, $3.12; and a machine operator, $3.40.

An unemployed mother on welfare might receive $400 a month in public assistance. A mother working at Selby might typically receive $320 in wages; if she is also receiving welfare, her monthly public assistance check might be another $270, for a total of $590 a month.

Since 1974, federal law has prohibited employees from asking job applicants whether they receive welfare. Prior to passage of that statute, management knew that many families of Selby workers received welfare grants, and it believes that the number is still substantial. However, because welfare grants are reduced by one-third when recipients are working, it is estimated that Selby's payroll saved $285,000 in local welfare costs from 1970 to 1973 and more than twice that amount over the seven years of the plant's operation.

Employee benefits at Selby include vacation pay, which is prorated according to the number of hours worked; a pension plan to which the company and the employee make matching contributions; and a health maintenance organization that covers doctor and dentist bills and most hospital and surgery costs and in which employees participate at the low cost of $6 per month. Sick leave is not included, but welfare payments offset the lost work time.

Selby's work schedule is a major benefit for working mothers. During the school year, they work from 8:00 A.M. to 2:00 P.M., which enables them to be with their children before and after school. During the summer months, they work the "mothers' shift," which begins at 7:00 A.M and runs for five straight hours (with a fifteen-minute break and thirty minutes for lunch). This schedule greatly reduces the need for day care. Women with preschoolers often receive help with child care from neighbors or relatives. Very few Selby mothers need to use day-care centers.

Students working at Selby are able to maintain their class schedules. They work at the plant from 2:00 to 5:00 P.M.

New legislation may substantially increase part-time work for welfare mothers who have school-age children. The Carter Administration's plan would create 350,000 federally funded part-time public-sector jobs under municipal auspices. However, it is hoped that more private-sector part-time jobs will eventually be developed, especially for people such as those who work at the Selby plant.

CUMMINS ENGINE COMPANY

Personalized Training for New Hires Who Lack a Basic Education

Cummins Engine Company is accepting and training job applicants whose reading and mathematics skills are at the third to sixth grade levels. The Cummins program, Long-Term Training (LTT), is one of the few of its kind in the nation. "One hundred percent of these trainees are economically disadvantaged," says Robert Wroblewski, director of personnel for the company's U.S. Automotive Group. "Most of them have worked previously at the minimum wage or below, often in seasonal jobs. When they come to us, they have poor work habits and don't know how to survive in the world of work." Long-Term Training has been in existence since 1970 at the company's headquarters and five factories in Columbus, Indiana. These facilities employ 6,500 production workers. Cummins is considering extending LTT to its plants outside the Columbus area. The managers of these plants will be consulted to see if LTT programs can be established at their facilities. "The key factor in these decisions is to develop people in your company who will manage the effort," Wroblewski explains. "You can't subcontract the program. We evolved LTT over seven years, and we have found that it requires a professional educator who understands the people we are dealing with, who is empathetic, and who understands education methodology and factory requirements. In other words, the program needs a pro on a daily basis. It must also be tailored specifically to the company's needs and to the kinds of people living in the area."

In early 1975, when Cummins was forced to lay off part of its work force, the program was discontinued for two years. Because the company was not hiring during that period, there were no job openings for LTT graduates. By contract with the Diesel Workers Union, Cummins could not hire new people until it brought back workers who were on layoff. Furthermore, Cummins has found that one of the most important factors in the success of LTT is having the program feed directly into job opportunities, and that was not possible during the recession. However, the program was resumed in 1977.

Today, LTT turns out about thirty graduates annually. In 1977, when hiring activity for factory jobs was low, LTT trainees represented approximately 20 percent of new employees. Between 1970 and 1974, some 100 people successfully completed the program. The program's goal is to supply approximately 10 percent of factory replacement hiring.

The regular training cycle is eight weeks, but it can be extended up to sixteen weeks for those who need it. There are two to three training cycles per year. Each class has eight to twelve members. "If there were more than twelve trainees in a class, individual instruction would fall apart," Wroblewski explains. "And if there were fewer than eight, the necessary group instruction would not be possible. Besides, much of the success of the program comes from a group process. The members help to motivate each other. They set goals for themselves, and they get a good feeling about themselves as growing, learning individuals."

LTT uses some programmed instruction and teaching machines for mathematics and reading. However, a full-time instructor always works with the group, and a counselor is available part time. Subjects include basic reading; basic mathematics; "survival skills," such as personal finance, relationships with co-workers, company expectations, and work habits; and shop skills, including an introduction to blueprint reading and machine shop practices.

For the duration of the training program, each LTT trainee receives 70 percent of the base starting wage. Once the trainees move into the shop, they become regular employees in entry-level positions in one of the factories. Some LTT graduates have continued their education and earned a high school equivalency diploma.

Overall, LTT's graduates are doing well. Wroblewski notes that "the people who graduate really want to succeed. They work very hard in the shop. In comparison with our regular hires, they do as well in job performance and in rates of absenteeism. We have a lot of anecdotal data confirming this."

Wroblewski points out that the factory job opportunities in the company constitute the limits of the program. But, he adds, these limits have not been reached. LTT is firmly established at Cummins. "Our program is not a frill," Wroblewski says. "To succeed, it had to be integrated into the company. It is no longer experimental. LTT is now a part of doing business, a part of our commitment to the community."

IBM

Bringing Jobs to a Depressed Inner-City Neighborhood

IBM Brooklyn's manufacturing plant started operations in 1968 in a seventy-year-old converted warehouse located in the borough's Bedford-Stuyvesant section. IBM's initial decision to establish a plant in Bedford-Stuyvesant was aimed in part at providing jobs in an economically deprived area of 400,000 persons, most of them black and Hispanic, where unemployment exceeds the national average. IBM hoped to set an example that would encourage other companies to undertake similar ventures.

There was another reason behind IBM's decision: to make a profit. The plant opened with a work force of 200, and its first assignment was refurbishing computer cables. Today, IBM's Brooklyn work force has grown to about 400. Its responsibilities have expanded to include the manufacture of advanced computer products, from cables and power supplies to computer display terminals and printers.

Each month, the plant is measured on its business commitments in numerous areas, including output volume, expenses, and adherence to delivery schedules to customers and other IBM locations. "We're proud, indeed, of the 400 men and women there who have made the plant a success," says Frank T. Cary, chairman of IBM. "It has been as cost-effective as any plant we have in IBM."

IBM Brooklyn has been helped by its close relationship with other company plants. For example, many of the plant's first employees received their training and their introduction to the broader world of IBM through extended OJT assignments at Raleigh, North Carolina, Poughkeepsie, New York, and other IBM manufacturing locations. Today, 79 percent of the employees come from the central Brooklyn area, mostly from Bedford-Stuyvesant.

As the plant's work load expanded, the converted warehouse, with its limited shipping facilities and structural limitations, became inadequate. A new plant is being built that will enable IBM Brooklyn to manufacture even larger and more complex computer products. The building, which will be completed later this year, represents a vote of confidence by IBM in the accomplishments of its Brooklyn employees and the soundness of the decision to locate a plant in Bedford-Stuyvesant.

IBM Brooklyn has become a truly valuable asset to both the company and the community. A five-man task force of economists and businessmen, created by President Carter, visited the location two days after the 1976 national election. They were particularly impressed, explains an IBM executive, because of the fact "that we had started off with the assumption that we would succeed and that, from the beginning, other plants and IBM customers would depend on what Brooklyn could do."

LEVI STRAUSS & COMPANY

Clerical Training for the Disadvantaged

In 1968, Levi Strauss instituted the Opportunity Training Program. It is designed to provide clerical-skills training for those under 22 and over

45, members of minority groups, the unemployed or unskilled, ex-offenders, the handicapped, and those on welfare. Trainees are recruited through seventy social and community agencies. To be admitted to the program, they must be able to type twenty-five words per minute (with errors), read and write English, and have a strong desire for a clerical job.

The trainees spend from three to six months in the program and are allowed to progress at their own pace. The skills taught include mathematics, typing, dictation, English, telephone usage, and filing. Trainees are paid $120 per week and receive all company benefits. Those who complete the program may apply for permanent jobs with the company. About twelve people participate annually. The classroom space and number of office machines that the company has allotted to the program are limited, and therefore only four trainees can be accommodated at one time.

The retention rate is about 80 percent for all trainees but only about 50 percent for ex-offenders. According to Joan McClintic, supervisor of the Opportunity Training Program, the typical ex-offender is not fired but leaves. "The problem is their life-style not their skills," she says. "Their friends can militate against their success in the 'straight' world."

To date, few handicapped people have been referred to the program. The company estimates that the handicapped constitute only 1 to 2 percent of its total work force. Consequently, a more aggressive program to hire the handicapped is being formulated; it is supervised by Gaylene Pearson. As a further step in this direction, Levi Strauss has just completed a survey of architectural barriers to the handicapped at the company's facilities.

Levi Strauss is enthusiastic about the results of the Opportunity Training Program. It would like to see more equivalent programs developed in other companies.

MANPOWER DEMONSTRATION RESEARCH CORPORATION

Testing Supported Work for the Hardest-to-Employ

The Manpower Demonstration Research Corporation (MDRC) is a tax-exempt, nonprofit organization founded in 1974 with the support of the

Ford Foundation and the federal government. MDRC, which is based in New York City, is supervising one of the most important and most difficult contemporary manpower projects: a three-year test of whether supported work can successfully aid four major target groups—ex-addicts, ex-offenders, long-term welfare mothers, and out-of-school youths from low-income families—to gain and hold full-time jobs. These groups, according to MDRC, "seem to be increasingly dependent on welfare and other forms of public assistance. They constitute the most resistant pockets of deprivation and dependency. For that reason, their employment problems are the target of the national supported-work demonstration."

Government-Business Support
for the National Effort

That national effort is being undertaken through a distinguished combination of federal funding and technical support, foundation aid, private research evaluation, and broad encouragement at the local level by the many businesses and government units that contract for the services of supported workers.

In addition to MDRC, the specific components of the national effort include continuing technical and financial aid from the Ford Foundation; funds from five sponsoring federal agencies (the Employment and Training Administration, Department of Justice; the National Institute on Drug Abuse and the Office of Planning and Evaluation, Department of Health, Education, and Welfare; and the Office of Policy Development and Research, Department of Housing and Urban Development); thirteen original project sites (Atlanta, Chicago, Hartford, Jersey City, Massachusetts, Newark, Oakland, Philadelphia, Saint Louis, San Francisco, Washington State, West Virginia, and Wisconsin); a principal research contractor (Mathematica Policy Research, Inc.) and a closely aligned subcontractor (the University of Wisconsin's Institute for Research on Poverty); local governments and businesses that have provided an average of 40 percent of the projects' resources in the form of work contracts; a total of 5,417 participants enrolled in the program through June 1977, including 2,235 ex-offenders, 1,007 women who had been receiving assistance under the federal program of Aid to Families with Dependent Children, 831 ex-addicts, 966 youths, and 377 others (former mental patients and recovering alcoholics).

The Supported-Work Concept and Its Techniques

Supported-work programs are an outgrowth of the *sheltered work-shop* concept, which was developed in the Netherlands, Sweden, and England, to provide subsidized employment and a sense of self-worth to handicapped people who were unable to find jobs. One key aspect of the original concept that has been retained in its applications in the United States is that the supported-work environment is indeed more sheltered than the environment in the private workplace. Thus, supported-work techniques are intended to accustom the worker gradually to the realities of the private workplace. By the time the transition occurs, the supports have been reduced to a minimum, and the individual is prepared to cope with the regular world of work.

MDRC offers the following definition of supported work:

> Supported work is a transitional, structured employment experience for men and women who have encountered serious difficulties in obtaining—and retaining—employment in the conventional labor market. As the participants gain work experience and establish an employment record, performance demands are increased, and they are prepared for placement in the regular job market.

MDRC emphasizes six supported-work techniques in its programs: peer group support, graduated production demands, increasingly strict work habit requirements, evolving interaction with the supervisor and with other aspects of the program, graduated difficulties of work assignments, and a graduated bonus system.

On the basis of its first year's operations, MDRC states that "for most employees, the quality and support of their supervisors are the critical factors in work performance and success. And for our target populations, supervision is *especially* critical." The supervisor is often the key to learning the content of work and the way organizations operate, two experiences that are essential to making the transition to regular work.

In addition, MDRC has found that it is difficult to wield supervisory control over people whose previous experience with legitimate power and authority has not been successful. For this reason, MDRC's guidelines recommend that "all supervisors be program hired and trained" so that supervision of high quality can be developed and so that supervisors will be sensitive to the special problems of the target groups.

The supported-work environment is one of initially lowered stress. Fellow workers come from similar backgrounds, and people work in crews, rather than individually. In the early months of the program, supervisors are tolerant of inefficiency, tardiness, or short-term absences. But then requirements are tightened up, and the stresses increase. Gradually, the standards and expectations get tougher. Mitchell Sviridoff, vice president of the Ford Foundation's Division of National Affairs, points out that "the hypothesis is that these people are simply not ready for employment until they have moved through the transitional experience of supported work. But this is not a soft social work program."

The work experience is also sheltered in that it is partially subsidized. In 1976, wages were between $2.50 and $3.50 an hour, depending on the project's location. This was better than the then prevailing minimum wage of $2.30 and represented about 75 percent of typical entry-level wages in private jobs. The level is deliberately designed to be neither too high nor too low. It is intended to be high enough to make working worthwhile but low enough to enable the management of supported-work projects to bid competitively for contracts. It is also low enough to motivate the participants to strive to succeed in the program and to find better-paying jobs. Furthermore, the wage rate should not arouse union antagonism.

However, there is some evidence that the wage rate may not be high enough to discourage criminal recidivism. This is a general social problem, though, not one of MDRC's making.

The Wildcat Example

The national supported-work effort directed by MDRC is modeled in part on the three-year experience of the Wildcat Service Corporation, a program in New York City initially sponsored by the Vera Institute of Justice. Wildcat's record is impressive: Some 13 percent of its supported workers out of a total of 4,106 participants through July 1976 have moved into the private sector. Of that group, at least 77 percent have held their jobs for one year or more. The dropout rate has been 42 percent, including 17 percent who resigned and 25 percent who were fired. Thus, 58 percent of the workers were still employed, either by Wildcat or in the private sector. By comparison, a control group (also in New York) showed an employment rate of only 20 percent. A comparison of incomes showed a substantial advantage for the supported workers. Incomes were roughly $6,000 per Wildcat worker and $2,000 per worker in the control group.

Criminal recidivism among Wildcat workers went down sharply during their first year in the program but started to rise in the second year. By the third year, it had increased to close to the level of recidivism among the control group. Welfare mothers and teen-agers seem to fare well; ex-offenders and ex-addicts seem to slip more easily.

What Kinds of Jobs?

MDRC reviewed forty proposals, and in June 1974, selected nineteen potential sites for local supported-work projects. By January 1975, thirteen sites were chosen for the three-year demonstration projects. All thirteen sites are managed by MDRC.

MDRC was uneasy about becoming operational in March 1975. The national unemployment rate was 9.1 percent, and the local areas in which the projects operated had unemployment rates of 12 to 14 percent. Nevertheless, jobs were found. MDRC believes that a number of reasons account for this: The scale of the projects was small, and they were built up slowly. Furthermore, the site directors were able to gain the cooperation and confidence of key local trade-union officials, political leaders, and businessmen.

Each project was intended to accommodate between 100 and 250 participants. By July 1976, the average was eighty supported workers, and that figure has been rising. By the end of 1976, the first full year, 1,500 workers were in the program. MDRC expects that figure to increase nationally to about 2,500 workers in the second and third years. It is clear that through 1978, MDRC is counting on results to prove its importance, not on size, which is small compared with the need.

What kinds of jobs have been undertaken? Up to July 1976, about one-third of the occupations were in some way involved with housing, including rehabilitation, repair, insulation, and demolition. But the projects are increasingly making competitive bids to operate city services or private contracts.

Most of the projects' workers perform maintenance functions in public buildings and housing projects, raze buildings, repair motor vehicles for local agencies, and provide security services for government buildings. Ex-offenders in Hartford are working in tire recapping shops, a filling station, and a printshop. In Washington State, former offenders microfilm state records and guard a state office complex. Welfare mothers, ex-offenders, and school dropouts in West Virginia are working as teachers' aides, day-care assistants in housing projects, and clerks in senior citizens centers. In Wisconsin, deinstitutionalized mental patients repair houses for the aged and poor.

In New York City, ex-offenders and others who have rarely held a job are employed by Project Scorecard, which audits the cleanliness of New York City streets on a regular basis. Crews of project workers are sent into neighborhoods to rate the cleanliness of curbsides, sidewalks, and alleys against a pictorial standard. The data gathered are sent to the Sanitation Department, which uses it as a managerial tool. The Parks Department also uses the project to evaluate the safety of the city's recreation facilities. New York City has since taken over the operation of Project Scorecard and hired its workers as regular, full-time city employees.

First-Year Costs and Results

The operating costs of the individual demonstration sites ranged between $500,000 and $1.3 million in the first year. There has been a strong downward trend in the average subsidy cost per person-year.* Total average costs fell consistently throughout the first year, rapidly at first (from nearly $15,000 in the first quarter to about $12,000 in the third quarter) and then more slowly. By the end of the fifth operating quarter, the average cost per person-year had dropped to $11,200.

This cost reduction seems directly related to a steady increase in program size at each site. Programs averaged 8.5 person-years per site in the second quarter, and 20 person-years by the fifth quarter. Those statistics translate to the equivalent of only eighty full-time participants per site, which is far short of the projected scale for most programs. With additional expansion during 1977, the average second-year costs did decrease further.

For the first two operating years of the demonstration, the workers' total attendance time for all the sites, including work and supportive services, was 76 percent. Another 8 percent of time covered authorized paid absences, and 6 percent represented inactivations or suspensions.

MDRC believes that "these figures are encouraging. They mean that a program can structure its organization's resources knowing that almost 90 percent of the work force will be accounted for as planned. Only about 10 percent is unpredictable on a day-to-day basis.

---

*A person-year represents the work done in a year by a single person during a standard number of normal working days.

"On the other hand, a supported-work organization must deal with over 20 percent of its total participant time unavailable to the program, whether that unavailability is planned or unplanned. The staff must be prepared to reassign and transport workers daily to meet the demands of the highest-priority work sites.

"The figures on absenteeism tend to corroborate what several program directors have concluded: that as long as a program has effective operations reporting, good communications, and adequate staff to ensure that regular tasks will be carried out, absenteeism will not severely limit its job creation opportunities or threaten its viability."

Other key elements for which first-year results have been computed are turnover and departures. For all participants who entered supported work before August 1, 1975, the average length of stay was seven months. (Figures ranged from four months at the Hartford and Massachusetts projects to ten months at the Wisconsin and West Virginia projects.)

By July 1976, 52 percent of all participants had left supported work. Comprising this figure were 23 percent who were fired, 11 percent who resigned, 6 percent who were separated (nonpunitive terminations for incarceration, institutionalization, layoffs, and mandatory graduation), and 12 percent who were in transition to permanent, nonsupported employment. MDRC reports that the proportion of employees fired was somewhat lower than had been anticipated. This was also true of the proportion who resigned. The organization believes that these figures indicate that, overall, participants are satisfied with the supported-work program.

Securing Transfer Payments

Supported workers receive a paycheck that comes from a variety of sources: payments for contract work, special government training and demonstration grants, and diversion into the wage pool of some of the welfare payments and transfer payments that these workers would otherwise be receiving.

The practice of diverting transfer payments to the local jobs corporation was first conceived in 1970, but it was not implemented until recently. Yet, even now, MDRC and the local programs are engaged in a constant struggle to persuade government officials to divert more income transfers into wages. At present, 20 to 30 percent of wages come from diverted transfer payments.

Supported-work projects will require continuing government subsidies, but to an increasing extent, they will be locally financed. By mid-1976, 40 percent of MDRC's costs were covered locally. The organization aims to increase that level to 65 to 70 percent during the third year.

Some Broader Questions

Mathematica Policy Research, Inc., of Princeton, New Jersey, and the University of Wisconsin's Institute for Research on Poverty are conducting research and evaluation of the three-year MDRC demonstration projects at a cost of $7 to $8 million. Using a control group, Mathematica is testing whether participation in supported work increases the likelihood that employees will achieve stable, long-term employment and an adequate level of income. It is also testing whether supported work reduces recidivism among ex-offenders or drug use among ex-addicts.

William J. Grinker, president of MDRC, states that the organization's broad aims are to "get a substantial number of people to function in a work setting so that they can get jobs and hold them and begin to break the cycle of dependency and destructiveness."

But Mitchell Sviridoff warns that "there are no easy or total solutions to problems involving the people we are dealing with. At best, we can hope to chip away at the problem, perhaps at 5 or 10 percent of it a year. We are doing very well in view of the fact that nothing else seems to be achieving anything of significance with this population."

The advocates of supported work realize that they must also find at least tentative answers to some other basic questions: How do supported work's costs compare with its benefits? Which work settings offer the greatest potential for successful transition to stable employment? If these projects prove successful, can they be replicated on a larger scale?

A demonstration program has a predetermined life-span. Although the research phase of supported work will continue until 1980, the operational phase of the national demonstration will end during the spring of 1979. MDRC's preliminary research findings have shown that supported work can be a useful tool of national manpower policy, that it is one strategy for job creation, and that it is one answer among many to the problem of welfare dependency. Given these indications, supported work has been written into the renewal of the CETA legislation now under consideration. The current plan is to continue demonstration and research efforts until more extensive research data are available. If such results continue to be positive, the experience will become part of an ongoing employment and training strategy for groups of people who are very difficult to employ.

MDRC believes that some important social factors will help to determine the success or failure of supported work. According to MDRC, supported-work programs do not take place in a vacuum. Their success depends heavily on the cooperation and financial support of existing federal and local program agencies, on the willingness of local employers—both public and private—to participate, on the receptivity of community residents to "another program" in the neighborhood, and on the hope that when the transitional period is over, employers in the open labor market will be able to judge supported-work graduates on their productivity rather than their pasts.

Clearly, cooperation between business and government on the scale that is essential to ensure that the supported-work effort will survive and prosper is just beginning.

OPPORTUNITIES INDUSTRIALIZATION CENTERS

Providing Training for the Disadvantaged

Opportunities Industrialization Centers (OIC) is a network of 140 organizations providing employment training and other services to members of minority groups and to the disadvantaged across the nation. Approximately 60 more OIC interest groups are working toward becoming operational. Each OIC is a complete community-based skills-training and community revitalization center.

Each OIC is an independent affiliate of Opportunities Industrialization Centers of America (OIC/A), a national support structure headquartered in Philadelphia that provides technical and administrative assistance to local OICs. OIC/A also provides training for management personnel who staff local OICs and conducts various national projects and studies in employment training and related fields. OIC/A directs most of its assistance to local OICs through nine regional offices.

What Makes OIC Different?

OIC is the largest such employment and training organization in the nation. It was founded by Reverend Leon H. Sullivan, who is now chairman of the national board of directors of OIC/A. One of its main principles is to provide training *only* where guaranteed employment situations exist. Another is the principle of service to "the whole person." It is this concept of wholeness that OIC believes is the key to its success. As the organization grew, it became clear that to be effective, OIC would have to contain certain essential components: recruitment, counseling, feeder (prevocational training), vocational and skills training, and job development and follow-up. Active recruitment was found to be the only tool capable of reaching the disadvantaged, the unemployed, discouraged, but trainable population. OIC recruiters actively seek out those individuals who do not possess marketable skills but who are or can be motivated to seek skills training. There is no fee to students for services.

In counseling sessions, applicants' interests and vocational aptitudes are determined. Personal problems are discussed, and steps are taken to eliminate or lessen them. The personal relationships begun here continue throughout the students' association with OIC.

The feeder component prepares students for vocational training. When Sullivan began OIC training sessions, he discovered that although some trainees wanted gainful employment, they had little knowledge of the behavior expected of them in the workplace. Trainees are assigned to informal orientation classes that provide them with the basic information necessary to make realistic vocational training choices. They attend classes in job-finding techniques, vocational orientation, personal development, minority history, and even adult basic education (ABE). In ABE, trainees pick up the basic reading and mathematical skills that may be missing from their formal education but essential for their chosen skills-training area. Many students earn degrees as part of this program.

During vocational and technical skills training, students master vocational skills that prepare them for job placement. This is an open-entry, open-exit phase; that is, trainees progress at their own rate.

In the final step of the process, OIC graduates are placed in meaningful jobs in the community that are related to the skills learned. Periodic follow-ups are made to check the graduates' progress, and additional services and assistance are offered when needed.

Training at the OICs

No two OIC programs offer exactly the same array of vocational training courses. Each OIC responds to the needs of local businesses, to the
needs of local trainees, to the requirements of a given locality's funding
sources, and to its own capability.

Business and Industry Involvement

To assure industry's commitment at the national and local levels,
the National Industrial Advisory Council (NIAC) has been formed. NIAC
is composed of key business leaders representing a broad spectrum of the
nation's commercial life. By providing counsel and assistance for national
projects, NIAC helps the nation's business community become familiar
with OIC and helps OIC enrich and update its programs and develop new
systems and ideas. One such idea has been the institution of a computer-
ized management information system. This project was developed with the
assistance of Pfizer, IBM, Allied Chemical Corporation, American Telephone & Telegraph Company, Sun Company, Metropolitan Life Insurance
Corporation, and Sperry & Hutchinson.

The council has initiated an industrial technical assistance contacts
(ITAC) system that assigns local executive- or management-level representatives of member corporations directly to local OICs in their area to
offer advice, expertise, and assistance to the local executive directors.

A complement to NIAC is the National Technical Advisory Committee (NTAC), an organization of management representatives who work
with OICs to help assure the success of NIAC-OIC projects. NTAC has
actively assisted the OIC/A private fund-development effort, has helped
develop publications and communications, and has provided workshops on
strengthening OIC-industry relations at its national convocation and at
regional conferences.

"Prescription Training"

OICs work for major corporations and small businesses by providing
"prescription training" for their personnel needs. Because enrollees are
trained only for known, guaranteed jobs, OICs develop close contacts with
local business to develop specialized training programs at OIC offices or

on-the-job training at commercial sites. One such example is the development of a technical representative program with the Xerox Corporation. Under this program, Xerox and OIC train individuals to repair all types of electromechanical equipment. Also, working with International Harvester Corporation, the Indianapolis Opportunities Industrialization Center (IOIC) has placed twelve local adults in International Harvester's Indianapolis plant. After a six-month on-site training course in engine repair and manufacturing, all twelve were hired at the ReNew Center in Franklin, a facility that rebuilds engines. In this training program, International Harvester provided classroom space in its plant, engines, blueprints, precision tools, and the expertise of its staff.

"When the program began in August 1976," said Kenneth Morgan, IOIC's executive director, "seven of the students were on public assistance. Had they continued to draw on public funds to support themselves and their dependents, the cost of the program would have been about $31,000 a year. Instead, the twelve students, whose average wages are more than $4 an hour, will earn $108,000 annually and pay their share of taxes. By providing training for meaningful jobs, businesses such as International Harvester can change people who are tax liabilities to their communities into tax assets."

"We realized about a year ago," explained Rodney W. Dunham, manager of the Indianapolis plant, "that our relationship with the black community was not all it could be. Although 22 percent of the plant's employees are minorities, the plant did not project a clear affirmative action attitude in the community.

"Because of the success of the first engine repair course here," said Dunham, other IH plants throughout the country are investigating the possibility of establishing similar on-site training programs. The advantages of on-site programs are many. For instance, the students get experience working in a real-life situation because the entire plant becomes the classroom and everyone in it a potential instructor. Furthermore, on-site training itself is more meaningful than other approaches because the students get hands-on experience throughout the course."

Structures corresponding to NIAC and NTAC exist at the local level and relate their activity and support to OIC affiliates. These groups are known as Industrial Advisory Councils (IACs) and Technical Advisory Committees (TACs). Firms belonging to local IACs map out a personalized strategy for meeting their immediate and long-term needs. IAC members help OICs to meet their training and employment goals more successfully by donating equipment, lending supervisors and trainers, providing on-the-job training and jobs, giving direct financial assistance, and designing fund-raising activities.

TACs provide a tactical approach to the problems of job training. Member firms provide technical personnel, supervisors, or operators of currently used equipment. These people either train OIC enrollees on the job or help OIC to develop a curriculum that matches the skills needed by the firm. TACs provide the one-to-one touch needed to assure OIC trainees instruction that relates directly to equipment and technologies in current use.

Many OICs also give classes in awareness training for employers' supervisory personnel. This facilitates truly effective two-way communication between supervisors and the minority group trainees with whom they will be working. These sessions teach some aspects of minority group culture with which managers might not be familiar, types of problems that might arise in the course of training or employment, and how to solve them in a mutually satisfying way.

Relationships with CETA Prime Sponsors

CETA prime sponsors are local, county, or state elected officials responsible for planning and administering local programs with federal funds authorized by the Comprehensive Employment and Training Act. OIC/A assists local OIC affiliates in establishing close working relationships with CETA prime sponsors so that program planning and service delivery address the needs of the poor and disadvantaged represented by the local OIC.

In fiscal 1977, over 136 local OIC affiliates received subcontracts from CETA contracts given to OIC/A for employment and skills training and related services. These contracts total $55,709,730, indicating that many prime sponsors respect the OICs in their jurisdictions.

CETA funds provide for manpower planning councils that bring together local government, business and industry, labor, and community-based organizations to advise prime sponsors during program planning and implementation. Many OICs have representatives on these local planning councils; they are appointed by their prime sponsors. At the national level, OIC/A maintains cooperative relationships with organizations that represent prime sponsors such as the National Conference of Governors, the National League of Cities–U.S. Conference of Mayors, and the National Association of Counties.

Performance

From 1964 to September 1977, OICs trained 477,498 people and placed 280,446 in meaningful jobs. Statistics show that 62 percent of these trainees were heads of families; 74 percent received some type of public assistance, including Aid to Families with Dependent Children, social security, unemployment compensation; and that 13 percent were veterans. OIC alumni have contributed an estimated $600 million to the national economy in tax dollars alone.

In 1977, OIC participants were characterized as follows:

Race-Ethnic Groups	Education	Age
Black: 65%	12 years plus: 43%	18 and under: 13%
White: 25%	9–11 years: 49%	19–21: 31%
American Indian: 0.5%	8 years or less: 8%	22–24: 52%
Oriental: 2%		45 and over: 3.9%
Other groups: 7.5%		

Sex	Pretraining vs. Posttraining Earnings	
Male: 40%	Average posttraining annual wage:	$8,320
Female: 60%	Average pretraining annual wage:	$4,784

Funding

OIC/A and its affiliated OICs receive funds from the Department of Labor, the Department of Commerce, and various agencies of the Department of Health, Education, and Welfare. Funds also come from major corporations, local businesses, labor unions, state and local governments, foundations, community groups, religious organizations, and individual donations.

RCA

Job Corps and Other Training Centers Have Strong Links to Communities and Local Businesses

RCA Service Company's Education Services, in Cherry Hill, New Jersey, is responsible for operating five Job Corps centers in various parts of the United States. These are federally funded residential training centers for young men and women between the ages of 16 to 21 who need education, training in vocational skills, work experience, counseling, medical services, and other attention. It is estimated that up to one-third of such youths live in metropolitan areas, where youth unemployment rates are highest. To qualify for the program, a young person must meet federal requirements related to maximum family income, previous employment, and age.

The sixty Job Corps centers located throughout the country were set up under the authority of Title IV of CETA. They are operated by private contractors, the Department of Agriculture, various nonprofit organizations, and state and local government agencies. Thirty of the centers are run by private contractors such as RCA.

RCA also manages other vocational training programs in New York City and Los Angeles that assist unskilled and underemployed persons through services in training and placement in varied occupations. In addition, since 1971, RCA has provided education-support services such as classes in reading, language arts, and mathematics; classes for the high school equivalency diploma; and vocational skills sampling for juvenile offenders in locations in Pennsylvania (Allentown, Aitch, and Cornwells Heights).

"We are in the education business," says Donald Naffziger, director of the RCA Educational Services unit. "I am pleased to say that the Job Corps Operation has been a good business for RCA; if it weren't, we wouldn't have stayed with it. And if we weren't doing an outstanding job, Job Corps wouldn't have stayed with us that long, either. We can apply our capabilities in teaching basic education and providing the high school diploma equivalent and vocational training to the operation of a center."

The Job Corps operation represents about half of the company's annual education sales, and 915 RCA employees are involved in Education Services. However, the Education Services unit constitutes only a small part of the overall sales of the RCA Service Company.

The cost of a typical Job Corps center averages $2,500 to $3,000 per student per year. Most of this goes to provide facilities, food, clothing, program staff, and medical facilities and care. In effect, the services provided by a center are similar to those offered at a residential college. RCA reports similar costs for each of its centers.

A major factor in costs and performance is the turnover rate. "Job Corps centers lose one out of every four students within the first thirty days," Naffziger explains. "During that first month, the students are deciding whether they like the program. We don't recruit our students directly. Most come to us through the offices of the U.S. Employment Service; the rest are referred by Women in Community Services."

Under the Carter Administration's new youth programs, the Job Corps is scheduled to double its capacity, from 22,000 to 44,000 residential spaces. With a turnover of two to two and a half times a year, the Job Corps will thus be serving about 90,000 students annually. In order to meet the government's plans, the Job Corps will be opening new centers and expanding a few existing ones during the next eighteen months. RCA has recently expanded its own participation in the program.

What RCA's Centers Offer

All RCA training centers offer an individualized education program that includes beginning and advanced reading, mathematics, consumer education, driver education, health education, and English as a second language. Curricula are continually revised to keep pace with the changing needs of the students. Prospective students receive information about the centers from Employment Service recruiters. When they arrive at a center, they take reading and mathematics tests and an aptitude test in each occupational training cluster offered at the center. And in a high proportion of cases, RCA finds that the students are qualified to take the occupational training.

A center's occupational training clusters are chosen on the basis of employment statistics supplied by the local offices of the U.S. Employment Service. This information is supplemented by feedback in the form of the job placement records of the center's students. Each center offers whatever occupational skills are in demand.

Each of RCA's five Job Corps centers has its own program: Tongue Point, in Astoria, Oregon, serves Alaska and the states in the Far West. It offers occupational training clusters in clerical skills, health, welding, construction, and telecommunications. The center in Tulsa, Oklahoma, provides instruction in medical, secretarial, and construction trades skills. This center has a steady enrollment of 200 students. Blue Ridge, in Marion, Virginia, trains 180 women from several Appalachian states. Courses in clerical trades and retail sales are offered, and the center's vocational training stresses medical careers. Woodstock, near Baltimore, Maryland, offers training to 275 young men. The curriculum includes welding, automobile repair, and skills required for the mechanical and building trades. Keystone, in Drums, Pennsylvania, offers training provided by the National Association of Homebuilders in painting, carpentry, and plumbing. It also offers a separate program in culinary arts. Keystone, the oldest and largest RCA center, has a regular enrollment of 670 and has been in operation since 1966. (RCA has run the other centers for two or three years.)

The steady enrollment of the five centers is 1,840 people, and it usually turns over two or two and a half times during a year. The average Job Corps student stays in the program just over six months. However, depending on the type of training, a student may remain at the center for up to two years.

RCA has recently opened three additional centers in Washington, D.C., Laurel, Maryland, and Chicopee, Massachusetts, which will serve an additional 1,325 trainees at any one time. In addition, 2,500 to 3,000 students are served by RCA's non–Job Corps educational services.

"The students need a lot of time, a lot of help, and a lot of pats on the back," Naffziger says. "They have been turned off by the traditional school. At our centers, we prefer that any student who needs it earn the high school equivalency diploma before leaving the program."

"For most students," Naffziger adds, "it is best for them to be removed from their previous peer group and to get education, counseling, and recreation each day." The curriculum includes a half day of vocational training. The education and vocational instructors are local teachers who have state certification; they are chosen by RCA to provide students with a well-rounded education program. The remainder of the day is devoted to voluntary tutoring sessions, student government, or recreational activities.

Some students work in a local company or organization. "We prefer to have the students spend a maximum of six weeks working away from the center prior to graduation. In this way, both RCA and the students themselves can evaluate their performance in a realistic work situation," Naffziger explains. "It is unpaid work experience, up to twenty-five hours per week."

Each RCA center has two components that link it to its surrounding area. One is the Community Relations Council, which is composed of ten to twenty private citizens or representatives of local organizations. The council is important because the students go into the community regularly and also because there is always some interchange between the center and local services. The second is the Industrial Advisory Committee, which is made up of interested business people who may offer the center some OJT slots or who will review the curriculum for the occupational training.

Good Results

The overall success of the Job Corps is usually measured in terms of how many students graduate and how many get jobs. (Other measures include costs per student and the number of students served.) About 50 percent of RCA's Job Corps students graduate from the program. This is 3 to 5 percent higher than the national average. The rate of job placement for all graduating Job Corps students at RCA is said to be 90 percent. (This figure includes those students who return to school and who go into the armed forces.) This placement rate is considerably higher than those of other CETA programs.

The center's performance must be viewed in the context of the background of its students. The student profile at RCA centers shows that the average student's reading and mathematics skills are at the sixth grade level, despite the fact that most of the students have high school diplomas; the average age is 17½ years; most of the students have very limited work experience or none at all; about 80 percent come from inner-city areas; 85 to 90 percent are minority group members; and 100 percent are disadvantaged.

Naffziger believes that when all these things are taken into consideration, the fact that about 90 percent of RCA's Job Corps graduates are placed in jobs is indeed encouraging.

RCA knows what happens to its students for thirty and sixty days after graduation, and the Job Corps tracks some of them (selected at random) for a year. On the basis of this random sampling, job retention among Job Corps graduates "is very good in the first 180 days: an average of 70 percent. It goes down over the next 180 days," Naffziger adds. "Some students return to school; others may decide their jobs are not right for them."

Ingredients of a Successful Program

Naffziger concludes that "the tone of the center is set by the staff, so staff selection is critical. You must have dedicated, human relations–oriented people. They must understand the students, but they must also run the center as a business. They must be sympathetic, but they must also create a world-of-work atmosphere.

"You should use what you know has worked. Our improvements come from management and staff training sessions, which are conducted quarterly and which are for all our program staff. We also conduct our own evaluations; our education specialist makes an annual one-week field visit to each center. In addition, there are government evaluations. For each center, we set quarterly program goals for the average length of stay, attrition, job placement, retention on the job, and the progress of students in an incentive system that covers progress in education and participation in other activities.

"It is also very important to work closely with the state branches of the Employment Service and the Labor Department. If there are recruiting or placement problems, the center must be ready to change the occupational training offered, the curriculum, or the number of students in a training cluster.

"Maintaining flexibility in working with students is crucial," Naffziger concludes. "By keeping an open door and an open mind, we tailor educational services to the clients we serve. Our product is people, and our centers need to make timely responses to the needs of their students."

3M COMPANY

Offering a Wide Range of Programs
for the Disadvantaged

3M's Factory Training Center program for the hard-core unemployed was discontinued in 1973. "We ran out of the kind of people the program was designed to help," says E. W. Steele, manager of recruitment and placement. "In addition, we had few hourly openings in Saint Paul. We have moved production work to other locations among our ninety plants. It wasn't feasible to move trainees to other cities. We didn't want to uproot people and subject them to all the stress involved in moving unless they could first succeed here."

The Factory Center was in operation from 1970 to 1973. For its first two years, the center was supported entirely by 3M funds. It received additional funding of about $45,000 a year from the Department of Health, Education, and Welfare, which was roughly a quarter of the program's cost. This assistance was first received in 1972. The center turned out approximately 150 graduates, and the retention rate was about 50 percent. "We had some fine successes, especially later on," Steele says. "Early in the program, we had some trouble getting people who would stay. All our trainees were certified hard-core unemployed. Some had problems with drugs or alcohol; some were ex-offenders. The problem was that they all lacked essential work habits. Furthermore, the community was initially distrustful of our efforts.

"But regardless of their backgrounds," he notes, "the majority of our trainees were people who were seeking employment opportunities." Minority males constituted the majority of the trainees. "Also," he said, "as the community came to trust 3M more and more, their cooperation made the program work well."

Both Abram H. Weaver, former supervisor of the center, and Donald Williams, former employment coordinator of the center, found that although some people failed, most of the men and women who came to the center "worked hard at it, and they succeeded." Williams offers this evaluation: "We are convinced that the people who come here have ability. Some of them also have serious problems. Nevertheless, they are capable people who can do a good job. They are proving that to us every day."

Anyone hired at the center immediately became a 3M employee and received benefits that included hospitalization, life insurance, holidays, vacations, and service credit. The trainees' pay began at the minimum rate, $2.30 per hour, with $.05 hourly increases after thirty and sixty days. Job classifications included general factory helper, general machine operator, and stock handler and packer.

Abram Weaver points out that the company had to teach much more than machine skills: "Because so many of the trainees had been without jobs for long periods and many had no industrial work experience, we had to help them develop an industrial awareness and the right work habits. We attempted to prepare them for taking the responsibility of a productive job. They came to understand why it is important to be on the job every day." In the *Megaphone*, the official company publication, 3M stated its conviction that "a man who is down, eventually will find his own way if he is given opportunity. This is what the center is about, giving the unskilled a chance to help themselves."

In addition to factory, clerical, or laboratory training, the new employees were encouraged to attend classes for two hours each day, on their regular shift, in remedial reading and arithmetic. There was also a course in English for those whose main language was Spanish.

3M had no trouble finding company volunteers for the ten staff positions as trainers, Steele recalls. Although the work involved no monetary compensation, the volunteers felt they would be performing a valuable social service. In fact, there were so many volunteers, 3M was able to choose only those with superior teaching and counseling skills.

Steele says that the program was well received by both the corporate management and the community. "The applicants were often handpicked by Donald Williams and by outreach workers from among people in the ghetto area. Others were personal referrals from churches and social agencies." No one was turned down for a job so long as they met the center's "negative qualifications." That is, a trainee had to be unskilled, have an income at the poverty level, and be badly in need of a job.

Weaver says, "We got personally involved with the people who came here. We often had to help them talk out their personal problems. We had to convince them that we were really interested in them and that they could, through their own efforts, become assets to the company and to themselves."

A Variety of Other Programs

Even as the center was phased out, 3M developed eight other training programs that today assist 300 to 400 people a year. Most of the programs are four or five years old, but two have been in existence for twenty-seven years. Together, they cost 3M an average of $600,000 a year.

An OJT office clerical skills program conducted in cooperation with local high schools has been in existence since 1956. Each summer, 3M employs up to fifty high school juniors. During their senior year of high school, the students continue to work half days for 3M. Students earn both wages and educational credits for their time at the company. A similar program for minority college students from the Twin Cities area was established in 1972. In 1977, it provided work for thirty-five students.

Since 1971, a summer employment program for minority youths has been open to freshmen, sophomores, and juniors from local colleges. No restriction is placed on academic field of interest, and 3M's Personnel Department tries to match each applicant's skills, experience, and interests with the summer jobs available.

From 1960 to 1968, 3M trained high school seniors to be key punch operators. Training sessions lasted from four to six weeks prior to graduation. 3M now maintains a clerical work-study program that accommodates twenty-five students annually.

A co-op program for training chemical technicians was initiated by 3M and the St. Paul Technical Vocational Institute in 1969. Students enrolled in the program work at 3M for six months: three months during the summer between their first and second years at the institute and during the three months of the winter quarter of their second year.

Since the early 1960s, 3M's financial division has periodically offered summer intern jobs to accounting majors who had completed their junior year in college.

Since 1951, 3M has maintained an active co-op work-study program with eleven universities. The college students accumulate one or more years of work experience with the company prior to graduation. The program was originally restricted to technical students, but since 1967, it has been open to nontechnical students as well.

A summer program for college students and technical faculty has been in operation since 1951. The company tries to give the students challenging, project-oriented technical work. Some thirty students participated in 1977, including about 30 percent minority individuals and 30 percent women.

In 1968, 3M established the Work-Study Program for students from Saint Paul vocational schools. The students work at 3M four hours a day throughout the school year, and the company has had 100 percent success in employing them after graduation. Twelve students participate in this program each year.

The company is very satisfied with these programs. E. W. Steele says that "3M has fully supported the programs, even during the recession. They are very successful both in terms of corporate social responsibility and in terms of recruitment and placement for the company. We have no guarantee that we will get the people back as employees after training them, but we are rather proud of our record. We get 95 percent retention in the various co-op programs and 100 percent retention in the Work-Study Program."

VOCATIONAL FOUNDATION, INC.

A Youth Employment Agency of Last Resort

Vocational Foundation, Inc. (VFI), placed about 1,205 of New York City's hardest-to-employ young people in entry-level jobs in fiscal 1976–77. Given the continuing erosion of New York's job market, the increasingly fierce competition for jobs, and the multiple handicaps of VFI's troubled clients, that is indeed an achievement.

"Our kids are the ones considered hopeless," says Walter N. Thayer, chairman of VFI. "They have no skills. All our clients have some background with social agencies, and many were once on drugs. We get the bottom of the barrel. We are an employment agency of last resort."

VFI's experience may be more extreme than the average, but it provides a vivid illustration of the problems and requirements of finding jobs today for teen-agers from America's inner cities.

Thayer started the foundation during the depths of the depression, when the job prospects of the average person, let alone those of a teen-ager in trouble with the law, were bleak. Originally, VFI's clients ranged in age from 16 to 21 years. However, the foundation has changed its focus and now concentrates on helping 16- to 19-year-olds. As a result, VFI's client profile has changed. The skill levels have declined, and the overall handicaps of these young people have, if anything, increased. In 1976–77, the average VFI client was 18.1 years old (88 percent were between 16 and 19 years old), had completed 10.3 years of schooling, could read at grade 6.7 level, had mathematics skills at grade 5.5 level, and had an IQ of 96.1. In 1976, 72 percent of VFI's young people were black, 23 percent were Hispanic, and 5 percent were white. VFI's clientele was also 75 percent male and 25 percent female. The foundation's records show that 9 percent had a known drug background, 39 percent had a known correctional background, 18 percent were receiving public assistance, and 37 percent had no previous work experience. Of the 2,085 youths VFI dealt with in fiscal 1976–77, 48 percent had a known correctional or drug history, and 77 percent were school dropouts.

George W. Carson, VFI's executive director, notes that in twenty-six poverty areas in New York City "the chances are pretty good that a youth may be an ex-offender or a drug abuser. Or a youth may be in danger of becoming delinquent, and that danger is serious when you consider the increase in the use of drugs (especially marijuana, alcohol, and pills), the extent of unemployment, and the dropout rate in these neighborhoods."

Jerry Ornstein, the foundation's associate director, explains that when youths are ex-addicts and ex-offenders, "it means they have had difficulties in the past. Their skill levels, academic knowledge, and motivation have all been impaired. Many of them have very loose or unstable family structures. The whole gamut of social responsibilities has to be imparted to them."

Carson points out that "many companies are reluctant to acknowledge that they hire ex-addicts or ex-offenders for fear of customer reaction. Basically, ours is a very nonforgiving society."

The Shrinking Job Market and
the Importance of Staying in School

To compound the difficulties VFI faces, New York City has lost about one-half million jobs, mainly entry-level positions in light industry and commerce, over the last decade. Many companies have moved out of New York City, leaving behind a very large population of unskilled or semi-skilled job seekers. Consequently, the competition for available jobs has become much more intense. Older, more skilled workers are taking the jobs that unskilled teen-agers once might have obtained. In addition, the small employer may choose to hire illegal aliens because they are willing to work for greatly reduced wages.

"You would think that with the intense job competition, youngsters would stay in school, but our recent interviews indicate that these teen-agers usually don't relate schooling to jobs," Carson says. For example, one youth told a VFI interviewer that "all school means to me is a lot of unnecessary learning. The only classes I went to were the classes I was interested in. I didn't think I needed to learn the rest of the stuff." Another youth said, "School doesn't teach you how to deal with life. I was never told why education was important to me in ways that I could understand."

Carson notes that "in some poverty areas in New York City, as many as 60 percent of minority youths drop out of school before the eleventh grade." In increasing numbers, 16- and 17-year-olds are dropping out of school and searching for full-time work.

The typical VFI client is not prepared for the job market. "The magic age for finding a job in New York City is 18," Ornstein explains. State laws prohibit anyone under 18 from working in certain occupations. For many jobs, it is necessary to drive, and you must be 18 to get a driver's license in New York. Someone who is under 18 can't work at night and can't work in certain 'hazardous' occupations involving machinery and power tools. Also, insurance companies can jack up companies' rates if employees are under 18. But the most serious problem is the attitude of employers: They say, 'Send me a man, not a kid.' That means that, as far as they are concerned, a kid is old enough to vote or go to war but not old enough to work. Or they say, 'Send me a responsible and mature person.' Employers expect the youths to stay on the job and do their bidding, but the kids won't because they still have a kid's mind."

VFI's Record and the Outlook for Its Future

By 1970, VFI showed lower costs than comparable government youth employment activities. VFI had also developed more personal and effective relationships with its clients, employers, and referring social agencies. In 1976, about 220 New York City agencies, many with employment activities of their own, referred those youths they didn't think they could place to VFI for help in finding jobs.

In fiscal 1976–77, the foundation dealt with 2,085 youths, conducted over 5,000 interviews, gave 823 vocational aptitude tests, developed 3,170 job openings, made 2,761 job referrals, placed 1,205 youths in jobs, and placed an additional 46 clients in training schools. Furthermore, VFI enrolled 252 clients in their remedial educational program that involved nearly 17,000 tutorial hours in basic reading and mathematics skills. As a result, 18 of these clients received their high school equivalency diplomas, and 6 entered college. "About five years ago," Thayer explains, "we were placing young people in jobs at the rate of 3,000 per year. Now, it is 1,000 or 1,100. The job market here may dry up. If *we* can't find jobs for these youths, who can?"

Nor is George Carson overly optimistic about the future. "If the current labor market conditions persist, will we be able to make enough placements in private industry to justify our continued operation? Our placements have gone down from previous years. In 1975–76, we had an 18 percent drop over 1974–75. This past year, however, we had a 10 percent increase in placements, mainly because of increased effort and the fact that we have been around for forty years and provide an efficient business service for employers. If New York continues to lose entry-level jobs in light manufacturing and commerce, our field of placement will just dry up. But young people who at least have received training in a marketable skill are in a much better position to get a job than those who have no training."

Is Small Better?

VFI points out that for each job placement, it must develop almost four job openings. And for each opening developed, the staff must make fifty to a hundred telephone calls to employers.

Because the foundation finds it easier to obtain financial contributions than jobs from large companies, it prefers to deal with smaller employers. There are several advantages to this approach: In small companies, relationships tend to be more personal, individual follow-ups are easier, and youths seem to respond better to a less mechanized, less formalized employment structure. "Often, we find that we must mediate between the youth and the employer," Carson says. "There are differences of values and often communication and socialization problems. Each side has to be explained to the other."

On the other hand, if a young person has real job skills and abilities, large companies generally offer more mobility and advancement. And a number of large New York employers *are* offering jobs to VFI's clientele. Among the companies using the foundation's services are Bantam Books, Baskin-Robbins, Chock Full o' Nuts, Citibank, and Merrill, Lynch.

Carson finds that "young people suffer from the same job-related problems as adults do: boredom, a need for more money, a need to improve their skills. Larger companies offer a greater variety of jobs and have room for some movement. However, without additional training, a school dropout cannot expect to move far or fast within a bank, an insurance company, or the offices of one of the *Fortune* 500 companies. But with tuition assistance or in-service training, mobility becomes more possible in such companies."

JUMP: A Program that Worked

In 1968, VFI was instrumental in organizing a consortium of engineering and architectural firms called the Joint Urban Manpower Program, Inc. (JUMP). Until 1970, JUMP was run as a strictly OJT operation, training twenty to thirty youths through the program. From 1970 to 1975, JUMP expanded to provide extensive formal classroom as well as on-the-job training in drafting to 167 disadvantaged inner-city youths drawn from VFI's client population. In selecting clients for this program, the foundation used special aptitude tests that were based on spatial relations and drawing rather than on previous learning.

Two aspects of JUMP were crucial: The first was the on-the-job training. In addition to drafting instruction, these VFI clients attended classes in remedial reading and mathematics, received daily counseling about personal problems if needed, and from the very first day, gained job experience by working half a day for the hiring company. As long as the trainee's progress was satisfactory and the economy held up, that youth had a job paying $110 per week. The second was postplacement counseling, which VFI believes is critical to a high job-retention rate. "Even though these youths were working, we found that they needed other supportive services, such as help with budgeting, punctuality, job behavior, and personal problems," Ornstein explains. "We learned that the more supportive counseling a young person gets on the job, the greater the likelihood that he will stay on that job.

"Our job-retention studies showed that the average trainee in our usual placements stayed on the job about six weeks. The hardest thing is to hold the youth on the job. Many times, it is beyond our control and beyond his control. The kid could lose the job for a variety of reasons, including recession, going back to school, joining the army, getting another job, or getting into difficulty with the law. It sounds horrible, but without postplacement support, 50 percent of our youths drop out from work in the crucial first six weeks. With closer support and counseling to prevent them from losing a job because of their behavior, our average clients will last three months on the same job.

"The retention rate for JUMP trainees varied considerably for each class. However," Ornstein points out, "the last two groups that received training in 1974 and 1975 showed retention rates of 66 percent and 70 percent, respectively, after eleven months on the job. This means that counseling in daily doses at work and in the classroom is much better than calling on the youth or the employer once a week.

"Although the unit cost per trainee is higher for this type of program than for many other programs, the benefits produced are much greater," Ornstein feels. "The applicants were not only being trained for a career; they were being taught how to work."

Many JUMP trainees were succeeding quite well, but the 1974–75 recession devastated the architectural and engineering professions because of the slump in the construction industry. By late 1975, VFI could no longer place trainees and had to terminate JUMP. However, because the JUMP experience showed that disadvantaged youths *can* be started on useful careers if they are given sufficient training and supportive services, VFI now expects to initiate a new JUMP drafting program in 1978. This nine-month program will involve twenty-three disadvantaged youths and will be funded by the New York City Department of Employment.

One Youth Who Made It

Jimmy T. (a pseudonym) came from a broken home and grew up in foster homes. He did not know who his father was. His mother was in Rockland State Mental Hospital. Jimmy attended a residential school for homeless children who are educationally motivated, but he was released as being incorrigible.

Jimmy came to VFI when he was 16. He was on probation for being involved in a robbery. "A 19-year-old in the Bronx used him as a point man in the robbery. Finally, the other guy threw a pot of boiling water on his back, causing third-degree burns," a VFI counselor said. The foundation got Jimmy a series of jobs as a delivery boy or messenger. Employers liked him, but he lost three jobs "because he lacked structure."

When Jimmy was 19, VFI got him a job as a typesetter trainee at $90 a week; he kept that job for over a year. Next, he became a metal spinner trainee at a firm in Brooklyn at $110 a week. He stayed there for two years. "The job required good mechanical skills, and Jimmy had great ones." However, Jimmy's girl friend became pregnant, and they married and had a son. They found that $110 was not enough to live on. VFI then got him a job at $150 as a bench mechanic. "He gets $170 now," a VFI counselor reports, "and they have an apartment in the Bronx. His work is exemplary, and he is on the job at 7:40 A.M. every day. We go to sporting events together, and he brings his family to VFI and to my house. Here is a case where we didn't let go, and our efforts really paid off."

Jerry Ornstein comments: "Jimmy was always searching for his own stability. If he had had a family, he might not have needed us. It took VFI, an exceptional counselor, a one-to-one relationship, and many years of patient effort."

The Lesson of VFI

VFI's experience with New York's troubled youths may be relevant to the situation of disadvantaged young people in other U.S. inner cities. In "Influence of a Correctional History on the Employment and Performance of Adolescent Workers," Jerry Ornstein compared three groups of youths: those who had been incarcerated or placed in correctional institutions, those who had been on probation but not incarcerated, and those who had not been in trouble with the law. The groups were comparable in age, sex, race, and education. Ornstein found that "there were little or no differences among the three categories in any of the variables when examined as to length of employment or number of various jobs held over a given period of time." He concludes that different groups of youths have about the same job performance and job-retention records, regardless of any history of trouble with the law.*

VFI's experience also shows that it *is* possible to find jobs for the hardest-to-employ youths despite the strong discrimination against hiring younger workers and despite the fact that most 16- to 21-year-olds lack marketable skills. VFI believes that the essential factors for success are sufficient funding, a reasonably healthy job market, on-the-job training, and personalized counseling, particularly after the young person has been placed in a job.

YOUNG & RUBICAM

Training the Disadvantaged for Advertising

Only one advertising agency, Young & Rubicam, Inc., has a government contract to offer a formal skills-development program to the disadvantaged. The program, which began as a pilot project in 1968, has had eighty-five graduates; thirty-five of them, or some 40 percent, are still with the agency. "The retention rates, performance levels, and promotions for

---

*Jerry Ornstein, "Influence of a Correctional History on the Employment and Performance of Adolescent Workers" (M.B.A. thesis, City College of New York, 1966).

these trainees are as good as, or better than, those for our normal hires," says Robert Haygood, associate director of personnel. "I don't think we would have stayed in the program if it hadn't proved fruitful before we got to those lean years a couple of years back."

The first seven weeks of this thirty-nine-week program are devoted to classes in English, mathematics, and advertising fundamentals. The trainees have a job from the first day, under a hire-first principle, and are paid $3.50 per hour, half of which is reimbursed from CETA Title I funds for the first six months. Further training consists of specific job assignments, and minimum raises of at least 10 percent are given at the end of the first six months. Trainees begin on either a clerical or a professional track, but clerical employees can switch later if they show aptitude.

Overall, the trainees' performance evaluations from supervisors have been consistently above average, and promotion records have been good. In addition, Young & Rubicam points to several unusual examples of rapid promotions: A 1971 trainee became the number-two media buyer in the Houston office by 1975, and a woman trained in 1975 as a machine-control clerk is now supervisor of her unit.

To qualify for the program, candidates must be under 20 years of age or over 45, handicapped, or a Vietnam veteran or must have been at or below the poverty level for the previous twelve months. The New York City Department of Employment certifies the candidates' eligibility. Some candidates have been receiving welfare or have come from the Work Incentive Program (WIN) for welfare recipients.

The agency has long had regular and extensive training programs for entry-level jobs in creative and media services and in account management. Thus, it was well prepared to offer similar training to the disadvantaged, and it also had a solid basis for comparing the job performance of regular and disadvantaged entry-level employees. This makes the good ratings won by the disadvantaged employees under highly competitive circumstances all the more impressive.

Summer Interns

Since 1972, Young & Rubicam has paid the salaries for a total of twenty-five college and graduate students who are recruited for summer jobs by community agencies throughout New York City. These students are mostly residents of New York's disadvantaged communities. Two criteria are applied: The student must need the money for school expenses, and the work experience should add to his or her occupational development. Although the company reviews the candidates' résumés, selections are made by the community agencies in which they will work.

ZENITH RADIO CORPORATION

The Largest Federally Financed On-the-Job Training Program in Chicago

"In the beginning, we were very hesitant," said Edward Youngman, a personnel manager at Zenith Radio Corporation's headquarters in Chicago. "In our past experience with government agencies, the reporting was so onerous that the benefits of participation weren't worth the trouble." But Zenith decided to proceed with a contract for 181 OJT positions for sixteen-week periods between May 1976 and March 1977. The contract was signed with the Chicago Alliance of Business Manpower Services (CABMS), the manpower and training unit of Chicago United, the business and multiracial coalition (see pages 49 and 57).

The money for the training came from CETA and was disbursed by the Mayor's Office of Manpower (MOM). (The city of Chicago is the local CETA prime sponsor.) Zenith thus became the largest single provider of federally funded on-the-job training in Chicago.

Minorities and the Unemployed

Of the 402 people hired for training by Zenith, 55 percent were black, 35 percent were Spanish, 8 percent were miscellaneous (mostly white), and 2 percent were Oriental. There were no American Indians among the trainees. Thus, nearly all the participants (92 percent) were members of minority groups. By comparison, in 1976, 47 percent (23 percent black, 23 percent Hispanic, and 1 percent other) of Zenith's entire Chicago-area work force was made up of minority individuals. Most members of the OJT group were semiskilled operatives and unskilled laborers.

CABMS received applicants from local Employment Service offices and service agencies in the city and referred them to Zenith with the certification that each applicant met three criteria: He or she had to be a Chicago resident, unemployed for seven days or more, and not previously employed in these specific jobs or trained in any government-funded program. No earnings criteria were applied. An applicant who was currently unemployed and seeking OJT training was assumed to be disadvantaged. According to Zenith, that assumption was usually correct. "The focus on the unemployed met a significant community need," says Roscoe Mitchell, Zenith's director of urban affairs. "For the first time in the fifteen years I have worked in Chicago, the city's unemployment rate was higher than the national rate."

How They Fared

The ethnic composition of the program's group of graduates equaled that of its entrants. Of the 402 OJT employees, 102 still held their Zenith jobs as assembly workers, 265 had left, and 35 had moved into other skilled or semiskilled work. The termination rate of enrollees in these jobs was about 65 percent.

However, when Zenith compared the OJT group with its regular hires in identical job classifications and for the same length of service, it found that the turnover rate for *both* groups was high: about 50 percent in the first thirty days. The average 5 percent monthly turnover among regular hires and the 60 percent yearly rate were about as high as rates for the OJT group. However, after two months, trainees showed a lower monthly turnover rate of 3 percent.

The OJT group also had the edge over regular hires in other areas. After training, OJT employees were better prepared for work. "This is our impression from conversations with operations managers," Edward Youngman explains. "Before the OJT graduates went out on the job, we spent two weeks with them, discussing tools, job techniques, benefits, and other work conditions." The OJT group was more efficient in adapting to new assembly line start-ups. The trainees also showed greater productivity. However, there are no statistics to document this.

Help from CABMS

Several times each month, for the duration of the contract, CABMS personnel visited Zenith to observe the training and audit company records. "I was impressed with the people we dealt with," Youngman recalls. "They cut through the red tape and helped in program design. They were quite knowledgeable, and that includes the people sent to do the audits. They checked that we did what we said we would do, spoke with the trainees, and gave us feedback on problems. The process was relatively painless. We kept our records, plus some invoices by individual hours of work per week."

Although the $3.62 and $3.72 per hour wage rates paid trainees matched Zenith's wage contract with labor, the OJT contract provided for Zenith's reimbursement for 640 hours of training per enrollee at $2.14 per hour. Additional special financial provisions in the OJT contract included special services, such as a maximum of 32 hours of training counseling per trainee at $3 per hour; up to 66 hours of job-related education per trainee in an off-the-job classroom setting at $2 per hour for those who needed it; up to 200 hours of instruction in English as a second language; special financial aid to cover child care (at $37 per week), bus fare, and a lunch allowance during the first two weeks prior to receipt of a paycheck.*

Wider Benefits

The trainees were not the only people to benefit from Zenith's OJT contract. The orientation procedures used in the program have been adapted and condensed for use with all new employees. Trainee supervisors attended a one-day awareness session designed to increase their sensitivity to employee needs by teaching them to interpret behavior. This awareness session, which was developed by the National Alliance of Businessmen, was also recommended for other Zenith supervisors.

"The program enabled us to do some experimenting that we wouldn't have done on our own," Youngman concludes. "I would be in favor of another OJT contract for Zenith."

---

*About thirty trainees required special off-the-job instruction, and sixty used the child-care allowance.

CONTINENTAL ILLINOIS NATIONAL BANK AND TRUST COMPANY

Employees over 65 Are Productive

Roughly 440 of Continental Illinois National Bank and Trust Company's 8,500 Chicago employees are 65 years old or older, and a majority of these are 65 to 72 years old and in good health. The oldest employee on record was 78. Employees 65 or older constitute 5 percent of the bank's Chicago work force. An additional 850 Chicago employees are over 60 years old; they represent 10 percent of the bank's work force.

Continental's special program, which began more than ten years ago, is based on the bank's policy: "We employ people regardless of age." The bank has mandatory retirement at age 65, but it permits its retirees to continue or return as part-timers earning hourly wages. Some of the employees over 65 work full time, but a preponderant number work part time, typically twenty to twenty-five hours per week. The over-65 group has an average tenure of three to four years at the bank, although some work longer.

Gloria Swanson, a personnel officer at Continental, says that "with employees over 72, we ask managers to judge whether a person's health could be endangered by the work. Only twice have we had to talk to someone over 65 about leaving — both times for health reasons."

Most employees over 65 work as cashiers, key punch operators, office clerks, dictaphone operators, typists, bookkeepers, mail distributors, and check, bond, and coupon clerks. They typically perform production, clerical, and processing operations. However, a small number are specialists who receive officer-level compensation. For example, an expert in international tax problems works sixteen hours per week.

Owen C. Johnson, the bank's vice president for personnel, is enthusiastic about the policy: "I can't think of another company that has an equivalent special program aimed at older workers. Other companies that are similar to us in type of business or organization — banks, insurance companies, and other service companies — are afraid of scheduling problems with older workers and are not so aggressive as we are in hiring them. Also, companies don't get social credit for hiring older workers the way they do for hiring minorities, women, or the handicapped. No government agency presses the issue."

Ready Work Force

The largest proportion of older workers are employed in the Ready Work Force. The force is a group of 250 people, 115 of them over 65; many of the rest are students. Many members of the force work unusual schedules, such as mornings, afternoons, or weekends only, with defined hours. Others sign up for certain days of the week and come to work on those days unless they are notified otherwise. Their job assignments may vary, or they may handle regular but periodic work flows, such as company payrolls or heavy volumes of checks. "We have a lot of peaks and valleys in bank work," a personnel officer explains. "For example, a great many part-timers work nine days a month in remittance, which is bill paying. We staff heavily and we expect a heavy flow."

Johnson notes that "we already have 1,400 to 1,500 part-timers in our work force of 8,500. We probably have structured our jobs for part-time work as well as we can."

The bank advertises for part-time workers and also relies on word-of-mouth referrals. But to reach the people it wants to attract, Continental has instituted a satellite recruiting program in neighborhoods beyond its immediate downtown area. Another aim of the recruiting is to diversify the work force with more minorities.

Referrals and recruiting also help to bring in workers over age 45 who embark on a second career at the bank; generally, these people have already had careers in the military, government, industry, or many professional fields.

Linda Lindsey, supervisor of the Ready Work Force, explains the procedure: "We advertise in local papers, offering two to three days' work per week in specific occupations — secretaries, typists, and dictaphone operators, for instance. We also rent space in temporary offices so that we can interview locally. We find that many people are frightened to come to the central office in the Loop; they are uncertain of the transportation and big-city atmosphere. We are looking especially for mature women who wish to return to work. They are stable and have good skills, they were taught grammar and punctuation in the old days. They are far better prepared than the people we see right out of high school, and their work ethic, dependability, and punctuality are much better."

High Praise

The older workers receive very high praise from supervisors for their strong motivation, dependability, and excellent attendance. "As a group, they are the most reliable, enthusiastic, and dependable people we have," says bank vice president Richard Gladziszewski. In addition, supervisors say that the performance ratings of older workers are as good as, or better than, those of younger workers.

On the basis of her experience with part-time employees of all ages and types, Lindsey concludes that "older people are just as dependable as housewives or college students and sometimes better. They come to work, not just for the money, but because they want to be productive. If they feel they haven't done a job properly, they will come to us and say so. They seem to care very much about pleasing, about doing the best job they can."

IBM

Retraining and Job Security Policies Benefit Older Workers

IBM has a tradition of full employment, and during the last thirty-five years, the company says, no employee has lost an hour's time because of layoffs, despite recessions and major product shifts. The philosophy behind this tradition, according to IBM Chairman Frank T. Cary, is simple and pragmatic: "If people are not worried about being laid off, they will be flexible in making the changes we ask of them." Thomas J. Watson, Jr., the former chairman of IBM, once wrote that the job security tradition "was not motivated by altruism, but by the simple belief that if we respected our people and helped them to respect themselves, the company would make the most profit."*

Full employment has been made feasible by the strong growth in the company's sales volume. From 1964 to 1974, the average annual gain was 14.6 percent. IBM makes every practical and reasonable effort to maintain steady employment for its regular work force. Of course, IBM *does* fire or demote people who are not productive. "We are not running a home for unproductive people," Cary told *Business Week*. "But our business has always recognized the effect that job security can have on the morale of the work force." Cary emphasized that job security does not mean less productivity: "If you operate in high job security without demanding performance, there would be a problem. But we demand performance" (p. 112).

Although IBM has been able to avoid layoffs, it has on occasion resorted to shrinking the work force during a recession by offering special incentives to older employees to choose early retirement, which company policy permits beginning at age 55. Workers with twenty-five years or more of service can retire and collect half of their annual salary for four years or until they reach 65, whichever comes first. Under the early retirement policy, those who are eligible for pensions will receive them, at a proportionately reduced rate. Since 1970, some 4,800 older employees have taken advantage of these special opportunities.

Education and Retraining

IBM's full-employment tradition is intertwined with its large-scale education programs. This is particularly significant in the case of employees who are retrained for assignment to new jobs within the company. According to the director of personnel resources, "employees can, over a period of years, work in more than one career path. Career changes become even more important when we must take steps to protect our tradition of full employment. When these situations arise, in addition to reduc-

---

*"How IBM Avoids Layoffs through Retraining," *Business Week*, November 10, 1975, p. 110.

ing hiring, we try to move work to places where we have surplus people. If we can't do that, we move the people to the work. If the people do not have the right skill mix for their new work, we train them for it."

Continuing changes in computer technology have greatly reduced the amount of labor needed for production and therefore have drastically reduced the number of production workers. Administrative staffs have also been cut, and people have been moved into expanding areas of the work force, becoming computer programmers and operators or marketing, sales, and service specialists. Because of growing sales, retraining programs have not been "all that expensive," Cary says. "We are growing. In 1970 and 1975, when we had an excess of people in manufacturing, we had a need elsewhere. If we hadn't found them in the business, we would have had to bring them in from the outside" (p. 112).

Since 1970, IBM's total domestic employment has increased by approximately 13,000 people (from 156,859 to 169, 694). Consequently, there has been considerable need for retraining and relocation in order to adjust to technological changes and the recessions of 1970 and 1975 and still avoid layoffs. Since 1970, 18,000 IBM employees have assumed new job responsibilities. Of these, 7,200 were retrained, and approximately 14,000 were relocated. During the period of greatest adjustment, 1971 and 1972, some 12,000 employees were moved into other jobs, relocated, or retrained.

In response to the very rapid changes that have taken place in the computer and electronics industries, IBM has developed one of the most extensive corporate education programs in the country. According to *Business Week*, "More than 5,000 full-time and part-time instructors in 200 domestic education centers now give three major types of courses: management development, technical updating, and job retraining. Some 10 million student hours are logged each year—the equivalent of nearly 40,000 full-time students receiving 15 hours a week in a 32-week college" (p. 112).

Since 1974–75, IBM has maintained a high level of effort in training and retraining, partly to prevent overhiring and partly to maintain its policy of promotion from within. At the company's System Research Institute in New York City, 300 to 400 engineers a year complete an intensive ten-week program to revitalize their technical skills. Small numbers of IBM engineers have participated in two other programs to update their technical skills.

Retraining and relocation efforts undertaken specifically to avoid layoffs are coordinated by the Corporate Resource Group at IBM headquarters in Armonk, New York. During periods of unbalanced work loads, the

158

group receives monthly projections of the work load from thirteen divisions and provides manpower balancing among those units with excess employees and those with openings. Costs of retraining are charged to the budget of the unit receiving additional employees. Where major shifts have occurred, the company has occasionally posted notices of career opportunities on bulletin boards, described them at employee meetings, or had company representatives solicit applications for transfers. IBM has also paid for relocation expenses.

IBM is also actively concerned with the education of employees who are nearing retirement age. Each year, about 350 people retire (out of a domestic work force of 169,000). A new retirement education assistance program was instituted at the beginning of 1977, under which IBM will pay for retirees' tuition costs up to $2,500 ($500 annually for up to five years). The program can be completed before retirement or can be continued up to two years after retirement. Because the early retirement age at IBM is 55, employees can first qualify for this financial assistance at age 52.

INLAND STEEL COMPANY

Most Older Workers Still Choose to Retire by Age 60

Under union contract, Inland Steel's hourly employees can work as long as they want to; there is no mandatory retirement at age 65. This contract provision, which affects all steel companies, has been in force for at least twenty years.

The contract covers the 18,000 hourly employees at Inland's Indiana Harbor Works steel mill. The 4,600 salaried employees (those not covered by the union contract) had to retire during the first month after they turn 65. If an hourly employee wishes to stay on beyond age 65, however, he or she must work full time; the company makes no provision for part-time work for older employees.

Despite this liberal age policy, there is a steady trend at Inland toward early retirements. In 1976, 446 hourly employees retired. Their average age was 59.4 years. Only 49 of these workers (10 percent of 1976 retirees) had worked to age 65. The majority of retirees were age 62 or younger. Among the 117 salaried employees who retired in 1976, the average age of retirees was 60. Only 31 of Inland's 18,000 hourly employees are over age 65; the oldest is 75. These workers must take an annual medical examination that determines their fitness for the work.

Any employee may retire with a full pension after thirty years' work regardless of age. The amount of the pension depends on length of service and level of earnings in the best three of the last five years worked.

"The message is clear," says George Yoxall, manager of personnel and training at Inland. "If people have an adequate income, they want to retire earlier than 65. In companies inside or outside the steel industry that have liberal early retirement plans, the majority of people retire before age 65. The criterion is whether they can afford to retire. Pension and retirement plans make the difference, not age limits."

RETIREMENT JOBS INC.

Helping Older Workers Find Jobs

In 1978, approximately 12,000 jobs in the San Francisco Bay Area will be filled by older people, especially retirees, through the referral services of Retirement Jobs Inc. When this nonprofit organization was founded in 1962, it had a single suburban office. Today, it has eighteen offices located throughout the five Bay Area counties.

"It is very difficult for older people to find jobs," says Harold Adams, vice president and executive director of Retirement Jobs. "Social security payments are not enough to keep pace with today's continuing inflation, and many senior citizens feel the need to supplement that income through part-time work. Furthermore," Adams continues, "it is becoming increasingly recognized that retirees form the largest pool of untapped experience in the country, and both business leaders and private citizens are now accepting this fact."

The agency's services have grown steadily both in numbers of people served and in the range of programs offered. The largest increase has occurred since 1975. Retirement Jobs filled about 6,000 jobs that year. In 1977, it doubled its output to about 12,000 placements, with a monthly average of 1,000 referrals. The branch offices play the major role in job search and recruitment and in placing applicants in jobs that are consistent with their past work experience. As a staff member remarked, "The state employment offices often send their older job applicants to us because they, too, find it very difficult to place people age 55 and older or even people over age 50."

With the aid of federal departments that administer CETA projects, Retirement Jobs has been able to hire a number of men and women to serve as outreach workers. They canvas the communities to develop job opportunities for people 55 and over. In addition, a quarterly newsletter is distributed to public and private agencies, citizens organizations, libraries, legislators, and municipal officials.

Retirement Jobs is supported by donations and grants from cities, private foundations, individuals, clients, and older workers who have found jobs through the organization. "When people get to know about what we are trying to do," Adams says, "they invariably want to contribute. In the larger cities such as San Francisco and Oakland, the business communities have been of tremendous financial assistance; in the suburban areas, individuals have responded in a most generous manner." For example, the Lockheed Corporation has donated an office in its complex in Sunnyvale, California, that is used by many Lockheed retirees and other local residents.

Retirement Jobs Inc. has other activities besides referrals. Under Title XX of the 1974 Social Services Amendments, it holds contracts with two counties to recruit, schedule, and match workers, especially older workers, to the homemaking needs of older and handicapped citizens; about 300 workers are providing homemaking assistance under this program. Another 400 are performing similar services in Contra Costa County under a private agreement administered by the Council on Aging in that area. These programs meet the needs of many older people by providing services that make it possible for them to remain in their homes and in a familiar environment and to retain the dignity so essential to their continued welfare. Such a solution is certainly far better for these older people than institutionalization, and it is considerably less expensive for the community.

Retirement Jobs Inc. has also developed several programs. that were begun by senior citizens organizations, civic groups, and other interested organizations. One of these is the Senior Home Repair Service, which is administered by the Senior Coordinating Council of Palo Alto. Through the council, Palo Alto citizens who are 60 years old or older can have minor home repairs made at very reasonable prices. The rates vary according to the homeowner's income, and for those whose incomes are very minimal, the city of Palo Alto subsidizes whatever costs are necessary for the required work.

SECOND CAREERS PROGRAM

Improving Counseling and Placement Services for Retirees

The Second Careers Program in Los Angeles was established in 1975 to help Southern California companies improve their retirement counseling and to open up more paid second career jobs and volunteer positions in community agencies. The program was jointly conceived by the Edna McConnell Clark Foundation of New York, which funds it, and the Los Angeles Voluntary Action Center, which administers the program. In 1974, a McKinsey and Company study was commissioned by the Clark Foundation to project the problems of retirement by the year 2000. The study reported that today's retirees are usually healthier, better educated, and more accustomed to high-pressure, highly structured workdays than their predecessors were. Therefore, the study said, retirees will find it increasingly difficult and undesirable to adjust to forty or fifty additional hours of leisure each week. Moreover, by the year 2000, the retired population could account for up to one-third of the nation's total population. The prospect of an increasingly large group of retirees who are able to work and want to do so led the foundation to provide funds for Second Careers.

Second Careers works with companies to help them assist their own retirees and prospective retirees in seeking another career in volunteer work, paid jobs, or new businesses. In perhaps its fastest-growing activity, Second Careers has already compiled a data bank of 3,000 social agencies that are receptive to using retired people and 20,000 volunteer job opportunities in 2,000 different categories.

The organization provides participating companies with the methods and personnel to support custom-designed retirement counseling. Second Careers also conducts periodic evaluations to see that the retirement programs are being adminstered effectively. The cost to a member company with over 1,000 people in preretirement status is $2,500. These service and fee structures were aimed at major Southern California employers. At present, Second Careers is working with such large corporations as Twentieth Century Fox, United Airlines, United California Bank, Atlantic-Richfield Company, Prudential Insurance Company of America (Western home office), Ameron Incorporated, and Automobile Club of Southern California. It is also making presentations to many other employers. In addition, the agency has recently added a consulting service for small firms at an hourly rate of $25 plus expenses. Second Careers has found that many smaller companies want to become more active in retiree relations but lack the experience and the staff time to do so. For such a firm, Second Careers will review a checklist of possible organizational activities and evaluate the company's demographics, past and present retiree activities, projected staff time, and corporate policies for an upgraded retirement program.

United California Bank has recently become active in developing a Second Careers retirement program. About 150 of the bank's employees retire each year. Under the new program, they will take part in a series of seminars, which are open to all employees, on topics such as financial planning, social security, nutrition, and exercise. A director of retiree relations will be assigned to give personal guidance on how to find a salaried second job, get started in a small business, or find a challenging volunteer job. The bank has already taken steps to provide work for its retirees. Nine to ten retirees were used on a rotating basis in the spring of 1977 to handle telephone calls during promotion of a loan sale to new customers.

Many of the participatory companies will also start an information and referral center that will provide specific information about government and community services and jobs.

XEROX CORPORATION

A Review of Company Policies and the Needs of Older Workers

Like a number of fairly young companies in new industries, particularly those in the newer high-technology fields, Xerox has a typically young work force. The average age of Xerox's employees is 35, and only about 100 employees out of the company's 55,000-person domestic work force retire each year. Nevertheless, corporate management recognized the importance of reviewing Xerox's pension and benefits plans. In August 1976, a task force was formed and charged with undertaking a thoroughgoing study of how well company policies and practices were meeting the needs of older employees.

Personnel staff from U.S. operations soon broadened the scope of the task force, as its title, Task Force on Older, Longer-Service Employees, shows. The group decided to consider a range of issues related to human resources and productivity and associated with older employees. These included alternative work-schedules, redeployment and retraining, midcareer counseling, preretirement education, and retirement planning.

An interim task force report issued in January 1977 identified a considerable number of proposed approaches and areas for additional study. The senior personnel executives who reviewed this report decided that they wanted further research on older employees' expectations, job opportunities, and work environments. This, in turn, led to an analytic review of the attitudes and concerns of Xerox's domestic employees. Attitude surveys taken in 1975 and 1977 were used, and categories of employees were compared according to age and length of service.

"We were expecting some unfavorable results," says Thomas Drucker, manager of management development at the company's corporate headquarters in Stamford, Connecticut, "but what we found was surprising. We found that the older worker was *not* significantly less involved in the company or significantly less well treated.

"Keep in mind our young work force. Nevertheless, the long-service older employees in our sample were not actively looking for the types of changes that we had assumed in the numbers we had anticipated. We had thought that our older employees might feel generally unhappy or disfranchised, but that wasn't so. Of course, they might still welcome some changes. But, for example, we didn't find a large-scale desire on the part of older employees to taper down their work hours or responsibilities."

Future Possibilities

The task force is continuing to examine a number of policy areas. However, its focus is longer term. Short-term changes will be considered only if they seem to be strongly needed.

Future retirement benefits. The company's Retirement Income Guarantee Plan means, in effect, that Xerox will guarantee a pension payout of at least 50 percent of an employee's expected retirement income, regardless of the pension fund's performance. The complex pension formula is based on an average of an employee's five highest years' income. Depending on cost factors, Xerox may liberalize the plan's early retirement features in the future.

Alternative work schedules. The task force has suggested using alternative schedules where appropriate, and staggered work hours are already in effect at the large Rochester facilities, where 15,000 people are employed. Alternative schedules, phased retirement, and part-time work are seen as consonant with the needs of older workers. One possibility being considered for the future is a pool of retired employees for part-time work. They would be used in place of outside temporaries. "The retirees know the company and know our procedures," Drucker explains. Another possibility (although it is not currently under consideration) would be to have a senior manager become a part-time manager emeritus to the person taking his place when he reaches retirement age.

Preretirement planning and counseling. "One of the clearest messages to come out of the study was that we weren't doing enough in the area of planning and counseling for employees approaching retirement age," Drucker says. "We have programs in the works. We found, however, that older employees don't like to be counseled by young personnel staff. We might bring in some older employees for special training so that they could become part-time counselors, spending perhaps 10 percent of their working time on it."

Xerox participated in a pilot program of preretirement counseling developed at the University of Southern California's School of Gerontology, and the company is considering using this program at its Rochester facilities. During the counseling session which lasts 2½ days, outside speakers and professional trainers discuss such subjects as retirement benefits, social security, investment of money, and adjusting to retirement.

Job security and retraining. "We don't have formal midcareer planning," Drucker says, "but if we move people out of their old jobs, we offer training in a new field. Also, we have tightened up on reductions in the work force because of a concern for older employees who have been with Xerox for a long time. Through a central control, we find other jobs for people and try to keep changes geographically limited. We use regular training programs and budgets for this."

ACHIEVEMENT SCHOLARSHIP PROGRAM

Second-Chance Financial Aid for Ex-Offenders

The Achievement Scholarship Program (ASP) helps young ex-offenders by awarding modest educational scholarships and providing limited support services. The goals of the program are "to explode the myth that those who go through the criminal justice system *must* remain losers" and "to show that many ex-offenders *can* become productive citizens." The Washington, D.C., organization, which was founded in 1973 by Helen C. Monberg, a Washington news correspondent, is a tax-exempt, nonprofit agency.

ASP pays each $700 scholarship directly to the college or trade school chosen by the awardee in his or her name. Scholarships are paid in increments of not more than $200 per semester or quarter. Scholarship candidates are recommended by parole and probation officers in the area on the basis of educational background and the candidate's aspirations and motivation. Awardees are then selected by ASP's eleven-member Scholarship Committee. The members of this committee are all volunteers, most of whom came from teaching, business, and public-service backgrounds.

As of September 1977, ASP had granted sixty-four scholarships to sixty-three awardees (fifty-seven men and six women). The 1978 annual budget is projected at $21,500, which includes $10,500 for fifteen $700 scholarships and $11,000 for on-the-job training for two awardees who will be trained to assist the executive director. The organization has been privately financed, largely by individual contributions. However, ASP is now seeking local business and foundation support.

Of the sixty-three people who have received aid through the program, five have finished their courses, twenty-eight were in school during the spring 1977 term, and two had gone back to prison. (One of these recidivists is continuing his education while in Lorton prison through a home-study scholarship from ASP.) Nineteen awardees dropped out of school, in many cases for financial reasons. Eleven either did not use their scholarships or had the scholarships deferred for up to six months because of financial complications.

ASP's support services include a course in study techniques, individualized counseling, and job placement aid. However, because of ASP's limited funds, these services are rudimentary. The individualized counseling, which is intended to maintain the students' motivation, is provided by the members of the volunteer committee. Unfortunately, these volunteers have not always been reliable in follow-ups with the youth. In a few cases, ASP has tried job placement, but the organization has found it difficult. The awardees themselves help to keep morale up. Generally, they know each other, and they have developed a certain esprit de corps.

At present, ASP is directed by 27-year-old Edward Hill, Jr. He was awarded a scholarship in 1975 and was hired as an assistant by ASP in 1976; he became executive director in 1977, although he still holds an ASP scholarship. Hill explains how the program has affected his life: "By providing scholarship seed money for my education, and by providing me gainful employment, ASP has become an integral part of my life. It has given me hope and purpose. I have learned to work with people from different walks of life; I have learned the importance of 'hanging in'; I have learned to expand and mature as a human being."

Hill is encouraged by the program's achievements and is optimistic about its future: "Of course, we went through a trial-and-error period, and the experience we gained was both painful and valuable. ASP is increasingly effective in its efforts to keep awardees in school."

AMERICAN
TELEPHONE & TELEGRAPH COMPANY

Largest Settlement Creates a Massive
Affirmative Action System

In January 1973, after two years of public hearings and negotiations, the largest civil rights settlement ever made in this country was signed by the American Telephone & Telegraph Company (AT&T), the Departments of Labor and Justice, and the Equal Employment Opportunity Commission (EEOC). It was immediately made a consent decree by a U.S. district court, granting it both judicial approval and judicial protection.

That decree has become a landmark because of the amount of money and the breadth of the litigation involved and because it was the first highly visible case that anchored affirmative action as much to sex discrimination as to minority discrimination. The affirmative action management system that AT&T, with its twenty-three operating companies, has built up since then is also becoming a landmark because it demonstrates both what a court settlement actually means and the problems and changes wrought by statistical goals and timetables as applied to the nation's largest private work organization (771,000 people) and the largest employer of women (401,000, or 52 percent of the Bell System's work force).

Job Stereotyping

Both the litigation and the settlement focused on job stereotyping by sex. EEOC charged that as of early 1971, nearly 60 percent of the Bell System's 732,000 employees were women but that they were highly unevenly distributed in the company's job hierarchy. Women constituted 1.1 percent of crafts workers, 1.6 percent of operatives, 99.8 percent of secretaries, 99.9 percent of operators, and 98.9 percent of service representatives. Although 41 percent of AT&T's managers were women, 94 percent of them were in entry-level management positions, compared with 50 percent of male managers.

To this charge, AT&T responded that it had led the nation in employment of minorities and women, that it was making affirmative action progress, and that it had neither created nor maintained these stereotypes. AT&T did not admit to any discriminatory practices in the settlement.

168

$45 Million per Year

The settlement caught other companies' attention, above all because
AT&T and its operating companies agreed to pay $38 million immediately
($15 million in lump-sum payments to 13,000 women and 2,000 men who
were alleged victims of discrimination and $23 million in immediate pay
increases to 36,000 employees). In addition, AT&T agreed to future wage
increases that were expected to cost $25 to $35 million annually for each of
the next five years, totaling about $200 million for the six-year decree,
which ends in 1979. But according to David Copus, who led EEOC's
litigation against AT&T, between 1973 and 1975, the first three years of the
decree, the Bell System had already spent some $130 million for back pay,
recurring wage raises, and promotion increases. An annual cost of over
$45 million compares with AT&T's annual profits of about $2.5 billion.
During the 1973–1975 period, some 33,000 female and minority employees were placed in jobs traditionally given to white males and received
wages totaling $300 million.

Not Enough Progress?

The 1973 decree did not end the negotiations and settlements between the company and the government. "AT&T is doing a fine job now,"
Copus says, "but they were horrendous in 1973. We hauled them back into
court in spring 1974, and that summer we found widespread violations of
the 1973 targets in eighteen of the twenty-three operating companies." In a
supplemental order, U.S. government agencies

> recognized that the logistics of implementing a Decree involving approxi-
> mately 800,000 people are neither simple nor easily put into effect. . . .
> Nevertheless, the 1973 reviews indicated that 1973 intermediate targets
> were not met for many job classifications in many companies. . . . [However,
> 1974] reports showed that system-wide Bell operating companies achieved
> more than 90% of their 1974 targets.

The agreement acknowledged that 1973 had been only the first year, but
the government said that nevertheless many targets had not been met
because of ineffective management and monitoring controls and
insufficient recruiting and overrides of the seniority system. However, the

court also noted the following percentage increases in critical job categories for 1973 and 1974: women in first- and second-level management, 46 percent; women in crafts jobs, 119 percent; blacks in first- and second-level management, 82 percent; and males in clerical and operator jobs, 147 percent.

10,800 Goals

Since rectifying its 1973 deficiencies, AT&T has been right on target in meeting the 10,800 yearly goals dictated by the decree's rather precise formulas. AT&T's computer system, Goals 2, is a complex interaction of these formulas; existing profiles for each of nine race, sex, and ethnic groups (five races and two sexes minus white males); annual targets; and comparisons with the external labor force. "The only unprotected group," an equal employment opportunity analyst notes, "is white males of European descent."

In 1976, AT&T missed only three of its 10,800 targets; that is, it met 99.9 percent of its targets. These targets are related to job opportunities, and hiring is way down for the company overall. In 1967 and 1968, the company hired 80,000 to 90,000 people out of about 1 million applicants; in 1976, only 10,000 to 15,000 were hired.

The fact that AT&T has virtually no discretion in setting its goals and that it meets virtually all of them makes it hard to distinguish the targets from quotas.

Making the System Work

Frank J. Peters, AT&T's manager of equal employment opportunity policy, says that "the most difficult problem was to set up management systems to make this massive program work. We now know, for every job category, every day, in every establishment, what is needed to stay on target." The Upgrade and Transfer Plan helps the operating companies to meet their targets. It allows all nonmanagement employees to make requests for promotion or transfer, and these requests are forwarded to the Upgrade and Transfer bureaus, which also receive company requisitions describing job openings. The bureaus match openings to employees who fit the race-sex-ethnic categories identified by the targets. "Selection is based on finding the most qualified person of the targeted race and sex,"

Peters says. "The Upgrade and Transfer Plan is central to the success of the program; it provides the necessary human resource pools so that we can meet our future targets."

Peters explains that "when candidates of the right sex and race don't fit the selection procedures of union contracts, mostly questions of seniority, then we must override seniority. The affirmative action override is mandated by the decree, and the supplemental order forced us to increase its use. The override is very controversial with the unions because it gets at the heart of seniority."

Three unions, including the Communications Workers, sued to have the override declared unlawful but were turned down by Judge A. Leon Higginbotham, Jr., of the U.S. district court in Philadelphia, in August 1976.* AT&T's case was turned down on appeal. The U.S. Supreme Court has not yet decided to hear the case. AT&T told the court that the override was used 28,886 times out of 112,518 hirings and promotions, a ratio of about 1 to 4. Even if the override is ruled unlawful, the supplemental order states that each of the Bell companies must then formulate new annual targets to achieve the same ultimate results.

AT&T's compliance system has many other aspects. Each of the operating companies reviews each of its work establishments. L.T. ("Terry") Dodd, personnel supervisor for equal employment opportunity policy, says, "The stress is on how well the establishments communicate affirmative action objectives to employees, how they monitor retention rates and developmental efforts—giving fair shares of training to women and minorities—while still getting the best people in the jobs. After all, we are still here to run a business."

AT&T headquarters subsequently reviews each company's performance. "We hold managers *accountable*," Peters says, "for meeting equal employment opportunity goals and for giving equal weight to other business objectives as well."

Several management development programs aid women moving from nontechnical to technical jobs. "Typically," Peters notes, "the opportunities

---

* The unions asserted that the government and the company have interpreted the consent decree as requiring reverse discrimination and that white male workers passed over for promotion by virtue of the override are "innocent victims." The unions contended that constitutional and legislative rights are violated by a remedial preference for classes of women and minority employees, rather than relief for those persons who are adjudged to be actual victims of discrimination. The case is *EEOC, et al.* v. *AT&T, et al.* Judge Higginbotham's decision is found in *Daily Labor Report*, August 27, 1976.

are in technical jobs, and the promotable females are in nontechnical ones. A woman who moves to a higher-level technical job will be supervising mostly men. She must get used to a new field, a new level of responsibility, and a new environment."

Statistical Progress

Table 1: Changes in AT&T's Work Force, 1972 to 1976 (*percent*)

Job Category [a]	Minorities		Women	
	End, 1972	*End, 1976*	*End, 1972*	*End, 1976*
1, Middle and upper management	0.9	1.8	2.2	5.4
2, Second-level management	1.7	4.0	11.2	17.2
3 and 4, Entry-level management and adminstration	6.0	10.0	44.4	43.3
1 to 4, All management	4.6	7.8	33.3	33.8
5, Sales	8.0	15.0	26.5	40.0
6 and 9, Outside crafts	7.7	9.5	0.2	2.0
7 and 10, Inside crafts	8.0	10.0	6.0	14.0
11 to 13, Clerical	19.0	22.0	96.0	90.0
14, Operators	22.0	24.0	98.6	94.8
All categories	13.8	16.0	52–53 [b]	

[a]Workers in job category 8 (general services, skilled) have been redistributed among other nonmanagement job categories.
[b]During this period, the average for women in all categories remained essentially unchanged.
Source: AT&T.

Table 1 indicates the extent of AT&T's statistical progress in changing proportionate representation within job classes between 1972 and 1976, a time during which its total work force contracted by about 3 percent, or 22,000 out of almost 800,000 people.

The sharpest increases have been among minorities in *all* categories, from 6.6 percent in 1967, to 13.8 percent in 1972, and to 16.0 percent at the end of 1976. Strong minority gains also occurred between 1972 and 1976 in the four management job classes as a group (categories 1 to 4) and in sales.

Women have continued to hold one-third of all management and adminstrative jobs. Clear gains were shown in first- and second-level management, but 75 percent of all management is at the entry levels, where women's share has remained essentially static. The most difficult changes to make are in the nontraditional jobs. Women rose from 6 to 14 percent of inside crafts in just four years. The female proportion of outside crafts rose from 0.2 to 2.0 percent. These are the pole-climbing jobs, where women have experienced 2.5 times as many accidents as men. AT&T says that although it is hard to find women to take these jobs, the targets have been met because there have been relatively few openings. The proportion of males in clerical jobs has risen from 4 to 10 percent and to 12.9 percent among entry-level clerks. The proportion of male telephone operators rose from 1.4 to 5.2 percent.

David Copus concludes that of about 150 court decrees in affirmative action cases so far, "AT&T is in the unique position of being able to say how it feels to operate under a *massive* court decree. The agreement helps Bell tell all its operating companies that they must meet the goals. It also provides the groundwork for knowing just what compliance means."

BECHTEL CORPORATION

Drafting and Clerical Training for Minorities, Women, and Disadvantaged Young Adults

Between 1968 and 1974, a total of 145 women and minority individuals were trained by Bechtel Corporation, the worldwide construction and engineering services organization, for entry-level drafting positions. Both

Bechtel employees and people from outside the company participated in the twelve-week program. Upon graduation, they were placed in Bechtel engineering departments.

In 1974, Bechtel joined with Youth for Service, a San Francisco community organization, to train sixteen disadvantaged young adults for entry-level drafting positions. The trainees were recruited by Youth for Service but were subject to final approval by Bechtel. The group included both women and members of minority groups. Youth for Service provided a warehouse site and fostered the trainees' motivation through individual and group counseling in job-retention skills. Bechtel provided the drafting equipment and the teachers. Those who successfully completed the fifteen-week course went on to jobs with Bechtel.

From 1974 to 1976, Bechtel also joined with Opportunities Industrialization Centers of America, Inc. (OIC) of Greater San Francisco to conduct a clerical training program for thirty-two economically disadvantaged people. An open-entry, open-exit system of enrollment was used so that trainees could stay in the program until they were job-ready. Program graduates were placed in jobs at Bechtel and at other Bay Area firms.

Neither the Bechtel drafting course nor the Bechtel–Youth for Service training program received any government support. However, federal money did help to pay for the Bechtel–OIC/San Francisco program because OIC is partially supported by CETA funds.

All three programs were highly effective because the training they provided was geared to equipping individuals with the skills necessary to qualify them for specific jobs. All those who successfully completed the training were subsequently employed.

Because the business conditions and staffing requirements of Bechtel change, training programs of this nature are reviewed and considered as the need arises. The company believes that this attention to current conditions is a significant factor in the success of the programs.

CITIES SERVICE COMPANY

Evaluating and Training Candidates for Employment

In mid-1973, Cities Service Company, a diversified natural resources company that has corporate headquarters in Tulsa, Oklahoma, instituted

174

the Employee Candidate Program at its Lake Charles Operations in Louisiana. The primary purpose of this program is to screen and evaluate prospective employees by paying them to perform a series of job-related tasks that are similar to the work in entry-level positions within the refinery. This process allows the company to determine which job applicants will make the most satisfactory employees.

Since the program's inception, all applicants for entry-level jobs have been asked to complete the five-week program. While the candidates are being evaluated by skilled instructors, they receive valuable instruction and hands-on training with tools and equipment. Cities Service feels that the program helps young and inexperienced people to make a relatively quick transition from school to work. Thus, both company and job candidate benefit from the process.

Recruits, walk-ins, or referrals from employment agencies are all welcome as applicants. They are interviewed and subject to a check of their past experience and activities. If admitted to the program, the candidates are paid $3.50 per hour for a forty-hour week during the five weeks. This period is devoted to familiarizing the candidates with a range of jobs throughout the refinery complex and with process operations, safety, maintenance, and laboratory procedures.

There are six supervisors and instructors for the program. Each is responsible for a specific portion of it, and each evaluates the employee candidates. These ratings are based on tests, interests, aptitudes, and overall attitude. The candidates are counseled each week about their ratings. They can be let go at any time during the five weeks. However, if their periodic progress reports are satisfactory, they are recommended for employment. The successful candidates become probationary employees in regular assignments and then full employees.

CONTINENTAL ILLINOIS NATIONAL BANK AND TRUST COMPANY

Outreach Program Recruits Hispanic Employees

In 1969, Continental Illinois National Bank and Trust Company was the first large employer in Chicago to try satellite recruiting in order to attract outer-city and suburban people to work in the central business district. The bank's affirmative action goals include hiring a greater number of Hispanic employees and upgrading their work status, and in 1975, the bank began to apply similar outreach techniques to the hiring of Spanish-speaking people in order to meet those goals. As a result of this and other programs, Continental doubled the number of its Hispanic employees in 1976. Joe Rodriquez, of the Personnel Department, is in charge of the outreach program. He emphasizes the bank's commitment to the principles behind the hiring: "We are looking for qualified Latinos, not as tokenism or because we have to fill a numerical goal."

Rodriquez goes out to Hispanic neighborhoods regularly. "Latinos are leery of coming to work in the central business area," Rodriquez explains. "They feel more comfortable in their own neighborhoods." He is often preceded by recruiting ads in the local Spanish press and on radio. Although he sometimes uses temporary offices, he generally sets up recruiting headquarters in two offices of Service Employment Redevelopment (SER), a Hispanic organization that the bank helped to found with CETA funds. (The name is taken from the Spanish verb *ser*, "to be.") SER offers programs in English and typing to a clientele that consists largely of blue-collar and unskilled people.

Because of some special problems, turnover has been high. In 1975, the bank hired 128 people, but over 90 left. In 1976, the turnover was lower. As Rodriquez notes, cultural traditions are a factor here. "Migration occurs frequently. People return to Puerto Rico or Mexico. To them, a family illness is more important than the job; it is the family at home that counts most."

CONTROL DATA CORPORATION

Strong Work Ethic and High Efficiency Shown in Rural Poverty Area

Wolfe County, Kentucky, has long been a depressed area. In 1969, when Control Data Corporation decided to build a small manufacturing plant for assembling computer peripheral products in this strip-mining area, it was the second-poorest county in the United States (second only to a remote county in Alaska). The town of Campton was deliberately selected from many possible sites throughout the country. The computer industry was experiencing rapid growth at the time, and Control Data wanted a rural setting in which to test its concept of developing assembly plants in poverty areas. Campton was chosen partly because its people were desperate for industrial employment and partly because Campton had an excellent pool of workers.

"The chief characteristic of these people was their desire to work," says William Craven, vice president of administration for Computer Peripherals, Inc., the company that now owns the Campton plant. "They wanted very much to work, and we found that they could be trained quickly." (In 1975, Control Data joined with the National Cash Register Company and International Computers Ltd. of England to form Computer Peripherals, and the Campton facility became one of the new company's three plants.)

"This is a dispersed population," Craven adds. "Consequently, people travel twelve to eighteen miles to work. No other employer of any size exists here."

Factors in the Plant's Success

Computer Peripherals says that Campton was a success from its inception. Because the plant was given a major product-line responsibility (subassemblies for high-speed printers), employment has been reasonably steady (except during the 1974–75 recession, when layoffs were necessary). In 1975–76, the work force dropped from 204 to 168 people, but hiring has picked up since then. Today, the plant has 198 workers. Annual turnover has remained at 13 percent since 1975, compared with an average of 35 percent in 1976 for all U.S. production facilities.

At first, managers anticipated special problems because the employees had a lower-than-average base of literacy and knowledge of mathematics and were generally unskilled in industrial work. Nevertheless, extra training costs proved to be only 5 to 20 percent in the plant's first three years, which is well within the norm for a new facility. "You always expect to lose money or break even in a new operation in the first two or three years," a Control Data manager says. "But at Campton, everything clicked almost from the start."

"We don't think of Campton as a poverty plant anymore," Craven explains. "It is a superb operation in terms of productivity, low absenteeism, and a strong work ethic."

Campton is the most efficient of Computer Peripherals' plants. A significant contributing factor is that it is an assembly operation only; it has no complicated engineering shops.

During 1976, Campton's efficiency level was rated at 110 percent, and its productivity was rated at 102 percent. (The rating formulas used were those applied throughout industry to measure output against earned hours in the plant. The efficiency formula measures only the output of jobs that are governed by defined standards; whereas the productivity formula covers all the earned hours in the plant.)

Hourly wages now range from $3.25 for entry-level production jobs to $4.00 for grade 4, the highest level of assembly work. These rates are considerably higher than others in the area.

Advantages and Disadvantages of Rural Locations

Why have costs been lower and productivity higher in Campton than in some urban poverty-area plants? Craven believes that "Campton people didn't have social problems, such as the use of drugs, chemical dependency, or substantial alcoholism (Wolfe is a dry county). They weren't hostile to the system. They are fiercely independent but also very good workers." Craven says that Computer Peripherals would look for another rural poverty site if it had the need for more production facilities. But at this time, the company does not plan to expand.

Why haven't more manufacturing plants been established in rural areas? Craven points out that there are, in fact, quite a number of small rural plants located in many states but that their existence is not generally known. He lists several reasons why the practice is not more widespread: U.S. manufacturing capacity has not expanded much in the last two or three years. Generally, industry still has an overabundance of plant facilities. In addition, high interest rates of 10 percent or more have deterred some expansion. Even before the 1974 recession, other factors have militated against rural expansion, including the difficulty of getting professional people to move to isolated rural communities; higher transportation costs; inadequate electric, telephone, water, or fire-fighting services; and a common assumption that training costs will be higher.

INROADS, INC.

Drawing Gifted Minorities
into Business and Engineering

"Our objective is to work with poor young blacks and Hispanics who have the potential for upward mobility in the corporate world. To accomplish this, we set high standards of performance and insist that those standards be met as a condition for remaining in the program. We also help these gifted young people understand that there are rules for playing the corporate game," says Frank C. Carr, founder and president of INROADS, Inc. "There is as much talent in the ghettos and barrios of this country as there is in any other segment of American society." INROADS is designed to help train that talent for business and engineering careers by reducing barriers to them. In this way, INROADS hopes to put more brown and black faces into middle and upper management and, in the process, bolster minority communities.

These ambitious goals were conceived while Carr was Midwest and regional manager for the publishing firm of Holt, Rinehart & Winston and were nurtured while he worked as a volunteer in Catholic schools in Harlem. Throughout 1969, he met with minority and business leaders in the greater Chicago area and with educators to develop the INROADS structure. He credits Leonard Spacek, chairman of Arthur Andersen, and Raleigh Warner, chairman of the Mobil Oil Corporation, with invaluable assistance in designing the program and in promoting it in the Chicago business community.

By the summer of 1970, INROADS had begun formal activities in Chicago. By 1972, INROADS/Chicago included sixty students. In that same year, the first group of women (eighteen) was accepted into the program to pursue the new opportunities opening up for women in business. INROADS/Saint Louis opened in 1974; new programs followed in Milwaukee (1974), Cleveland (1976), and Pittsburgh (1977). An INROADS program is scheduled to open in Nashville in 1978. Engineering programs were initiated in Chicago and Milwaukee in 1975, and a new business program is scheduled to begin in Cleveland in early 1978.

Most of the organization's income is used to pay for its staff, which is responsible for the recruiting and the year-round counseling and training programs. Sponsoring companies pay INROADS $1,600 per student per year to cover these costs. The staff is all black or Hispanic. "In each city, we are run by minorities for minorities," Carr says. "I am the exception, the showcase white."

The job of selling the INROADS concept, Carr says, has become somewhat easier as INROADS has acquired a reputation for developing good college graduates. He continues to find a reservoir of goodwill and the resources and ability to get things done in the corporate world. For this reason, INROADS has projected expansion to fifteen cities in the next decade.

INROADS is often asked why it concentrates *only* on black and Hispanic students to major in business or engineering in college. Carr explains that INROADS believes "companies are starved for talented minority individuals who can rise to higher levels. Companies, like other institutions, are pyramids; the higher the individual rises, the fewer the jobs and the more competitive the requirements. That's what makes good work records and credentials so very important. We are trying to put winners in there. It is a slow process and takes lots of patience."

INROADS is only one of a number of organizations devoted to developing minority professionals. A nationwide effort is under way to increase the number of minority engineers. Yet, in spite of these efforts, only 2 percent of current engineering graduates are minority individuals (an increase of only 1 percent).

Carr notes that although efforts to develop talented minority graduates who can succeed in business and the professions are still inadequate, it is vital to draw minority youths away from overcrowded fields such as teaching and social work and instead attract them specifically to those fields where jobs exist and where a disproportionate share of the power and influence in American society rests. But unless candidates are carefully selected and trained, dropout rates in college can be very high.

Today, 150 corporations sponsor 275 college students in INROADS programs; approximately half the students are women. On the average, a participating company sponsors two students. In addition, 195 young people from the eighth grade through high school receive supplementary training in reading, writing, arithmetic, mathematics, and laboratory sciences that gives them a head start in the direction of careers in engineering, accounting, and business.

INROADS finds that its students usually qualify for near-maximum college grants of $1,500 each from the state and federal governments. Often, the students work each summer at their sponsoring companies. If they live at home, their income after expenses may add up to $1,500, and INROADS helps them budget their money. Generally, they need only small college loans.

180

Obligations

What are the obligations of students to companies, and vice versa? The parties, says Carr, "aren't indentured to each other, but we try to achieve a marriage. After all, the companies are paying $1,600 a year for the student's special training. The better the results, the more chance INROADS has of keeping the companies and therefore the greater the probability that other students will be offered similar opportunities." INROADS/Chicago, now in its seventh year, reports that 70 percent of its twenty-two current graduates are employed by their sponsors.

Some of the companies also offer personal help. In Chicago, senior accountants from Arthur Andersen tutor their INROADS accounting majors before final exams. Seven major companies in Cleveland drill student applicants in job interview techniques and also discuss career opportunities in business. Participating company representatives are selected on the basis of backgrounds similar to those of the students.

Get Them Young

INROADS is deliberately increasing its focus on precollege education for youths between the ages of 13 and 18. "The reason is the need for acculturation as well as a sound academic foundation," Carr explains. "We have found that it is unrealistic simply to recruit minority students right out of college when they have been experiencing mainly an all-black or all-brown world and have also received inadequate academic preparation. We have been backing up to work with teen-agers in the early grades of high school in order to help them develop the skills and attitudes they will need later." For example, in 1975 and 1976, INROADS/Chicago was unable to find enough minority college freshmen with the academic preparation necessary to succeed in a college of engineering. It therefore enrolled sixty-five students from the ninth to eleventh grades in a year-round program at the Illinois Institute of Technology. During the summer, mornings are devoted to reading, writing, and mathematics; afternoons are reserved for engineering projects directed by the institute's faculty and corporate engineers loaned to the INROADS programs. During the academic year, classes are held on thirty Saturdays.

This is the largest preengineering program sponsored by INROADS. The others are in Milwaukee (forty-five students) and in Saint Louis (sixty students). The criteria for selection include aptitude in mathematics and science, problem-solving ability, teacher and counselor recommendations, and parental support.

Coping with the Demands of Professional Life

INROADS also provides a formal training program covering nonacademic skills and attitudes. Up to sixty hours a year of instruction are devoted to how to dress, handle conversation, manage time, set goals, make decisions, negotiate, behave during a job interview, and budget money. These skills are taught in small workshops, generally by corporate volunteers. They are then practiced at special monthly career dinners attended by students, executives from the corporate sponsors, and INROADS staff. Skills seminars are also given on college campuses.

Who Is Eligible?

The majority of INROADS' clients are members of minority groups. However, to date, the organization has not been able to recruit any Native Americans. And although it prefers to serve the poor, INROADS will also accept middle-class students who are in need of the training it can provide, usually because of the very stringent academic or social demands of certain occupations.

INROADS has not compiled a socioeconomic profile of its students as a group, nor does it set any sharp rules about family income. However, a breakdown by income of thirty INROADS preengineering students at Marquette University in Milwaukee shows that about fifteen come from families with incomes of $6,000 or less, eight or nine come from families with incomes under $12,000, and the balance (six or seven) are from large families (up to twelve children) with incomes under $18,000.

In Chicago, INROADS is recruiting fewer young people from families with incomes of $6,000 or less. "The deprivation among that group in Chicago is so great that we don't think we can help," Carr explains. "Also, we don't know how to touch the hard-core unemployed youths, the ones who are not motivated by the work ethic."

What Makes INROADS Work?

Supporters cite a number of important reasons for the success of INROADS. Silas Cathcart, a member of the advisory board in Chicago and chairman of Illinois Tool Works, says, "INROADS has been effective because it has staying power. It follows through with the students along their career paths and provides them with individual attention. Quality is what distinguishes this program, not quantity. We must work with small numbers in order to ensure success."

Michael Mahoney, an industrial-relations vice president of Heil Co., Milwaukee, is impressed with two factors: "The staff insists on a high level of performance on the part of INROADS students, and their parents give them strong guidance and drive."

Gerardo Orellana, manager of equal employment opportunity for TRW and an INROADS/Cleveland board member, says, "I find INROADS appealing because it leaves the primary initiative to the students. They pick their own careers, and they follow through on their own. They are given a hand but not a handout. The coordinators have a good grasp of the counseling techniques and resources necessary to ease the problems facing inner-city youths."

Miguel Lopez, a recent alumnus, now works for Commonwealth Edison Company. He says, "INROADS helped give me the incentive to finish school and to perform at my best. I wanted to prove to myself and to my INROADS coordinator that I could do well."

NATIONAL ADVISORY COUNCIL ON MINORITIES IN ENGINEERING

Bringing More Minority Students into Engineering

The National Advisory Council on Minorities in Engineering (NACME) is a unique partnership of business, education, government, and the minority community. It was created in 1973 by the National Academy of Engineering, which is leading and coordinating the national effort to increase the number of minority engineering graduates tenfold in the next decade. That effort, which involves many sectors of American society, was inspired by the fact that blacks, Mexican-Americans, Puerto Ricans, and Native Americans are significantly underrepresented in the engineering profession, compared with the general population.

The inadequate supply of minority engineers poses a major problem for technically based corporations and government agencies that are pursuing affirmative action efforts at the professional and managerial levels. The numbers are also well short of proportional population representation (parity). Before the academy assumed leadership of the effort, less than 1 percent of the nation's engineering graduates were members of minority groups. The proportion of 1976 graduates was close to 4 percent. NACME's interim goal is for minorities to achieve parity with non-minority engineering students by 1982. Based on the number of minority students who will reach college age by that date, they should then represent 18 percent (14,000) of all entering freshmen engineering students.

Since September 1976, NACME has also been committed to stimulating and expanding community-based activities by its member organizations to reach minority group students in the junior and senior high schools. The purpose of these precollege programs is to enlarge significantly the pool of academically prepared and motivated minority students who might choose engineering as a viable career.

NACME members are well positioned to implement programs at the community level. They include chief corporate executives of major technological companies, leaders of minority community organizations, presidents of outstanding engineering colleges, and government advisors. At present, there are thirty-eight industrial members out of a total NACME membership of about fifty. Industrial members have major employment locations in every state except Hawaii and in more than 700 individual communities. Nonindustrial members have offices, chapters, and affiliates around the country. More than 100 local programs are already under way, largely through the efforts of individual NACME organizations or groups of member organizations working cooperatively in a single community. These programs identify students with potential and interest, inform them of the opportunities that exist in engineering, motivate their parents to be supportive and interested, establish follow-up programs to encourage students throughout their high school careers, and assist in making available the scholarship funds that these students must have in order to enroll in engineering programs in college. NACME and the academy were instrumental in establishing the National Fund for Minority Engineering Students, Inc., which provided some $2.75 million to students in seventy colleges and universities in 1977.

NACME provides counsel to the president of the National Academy of Engineering and to the chairman of the academy's Committee on Minorities in Engineering, which formulates policy for the academy. It also provides financial support for that committee through annual contributions from industrial members.

By enlarging the available pool of academically prepared and motivated young people, NACME hopes to meet its goals for parity representation among enrollees and graduates and eventually in the engineering profession itself. But the program has even more significant implications: Because engineering can be an important educational background for high-level management positions, the work of NACME and other organizations will increase the representation of minorities in key management and policy-making positions in industry and government in the years to come.

SEARS, ROEBUCK AND COMPANY

Massive Voluntary Affirmative Action Program

In August 1973, William H. Brown III, then chairman of the Equal Employment Opportunity Commission (EEOC), issued a commissioner's charge of discrimination "on a national scale" in all aspects of employment against four giant companies (Sears, Roebuck; General Motors; Ford; and General Electric) and one union (International Brotherhood of Electrical Workers). These were to be cases on which the commission's staff would concentrate its efforts to settle or litigate. More than four years later, the charges remain unresolved.

Sears, Roebuck, the nation's largest retail employer, has had an affirmative action program since 1968. It is a *voluntary* compliance program. And in its sweeping long-range goals, its mandatory requirements wherever groups are underrepresented in the Sears work force, its comprehensive implementation system, and the rapid proportional gains for women and minority individuals in most job categories that it has effected in the last few years, it matches any court-imposed plan in the country.

At the time the commissioner's charge was issued, Sears accelerated and recast its existing affirmative action program to include a pioneering element, mandatory achievement of goals (MAG), that has increased the company's statistical rate of progress. For that progress, Sears won the 1975 EEO Award from *Business and Society Review*, a journal devoted to corporate social responsibility.

How MAG Works

MAG requires positive numerical results in each job category in which minorities, women, or men are underrepresented. Consequently, it has speeded up year-to-year changes in the company's work force (see Table 1).

Table 1: Changes in the Sears Work Force, 1966 to 1976 *(percent)*

Equal Employment Opportunity Categories	Women		Minorities	
	1966 [a]	1976 [b]	1966 [a]	1976 [b]
Officials and managers	20.0	33.5	1.4	8.8
Professionals [c]	19.2	43.8	1.6	8.3
Technicians [c]	48.1	45.3	3.3	15.2
Sales workers	56.9	63.2	5.3	17.1
Office and clerical	86.0	87.4	5.9	18.7
Crafts workers	3.8	6.8	6.4	14.8
Operatives	12.0	12.6	18.3	26.6
Laborers	34.3	28.9	25.2	30.2
Service workers	32.3	41.2	47.5	37.4
All categories	50.7	55.0	8.7	18.9

[a] Figures are for February 1966.
[b] Figures are for July 1976.
[c] Some reclassification of job titles has occurred in these categories since 1969.
Source: Sears, Roebuck and Company, *Annual Report* (1976).

Under MAG, unit managers must maintain the existing representation of minorities and women when filling job openings. An even more important requirement is that 50 percent of all job openings are to be filled by members of underrepresented groups; however, the manager has the freedom to choose from among the various underrepresented groups. For categories of nontraditional jobs, such as male clericals or female automotive mechanics, if qualified candidates from underrepresented groups are in short supply, the requirement is reduced to 20 percent.

A local manager can deviate from these requirements only if he or she has first documented a good-faith effort to hire from these groups and received formal approval to bypass. If a candidate is truly unavailable, the manager can then bypass the MAG ratio. In the four years that MAG has been in effect, hundreds of such bypasses have been permitted. However, the total is small in comparison with the 150,000 or more people that Sears hires each year in accordance with MAG requirements.

According to Ray J. Graham, MAG's creator and Sears's director of equal employment opportunity, MAG avoids being an illegal quota system by virtue of its flexibility and the inclusion of the bypass provision as a safety valve to cover those situations in which qualified candidates from underrepresented groups cannot be found. "However," Graham says, "Sears feels that such candidates generally *can* be found."

According to Graham, the difference between MAG and other affirmative action programs is that MAG does not rely on good intentions or on guessing about job openings in order to set short-range goals. Instead, the existence and extent of underrepresentation in fifty job categories is established for individual Sears facilities by reference to group proportions in the nation, the surrounding metropolitan area, and the smaller "hiring/trading area" (the area surrounding a store from which employees and customers are drawn).

Notable Gains for Women and Minorities

Sears's progress in increasing the number of women in supervisory jobs and the number of minority group members in most job categories was notably greater than the national averages (see Table 2). In 1965, women held 20 percent of the company's supervisory jobs; in mid-1976, they held 33.5 percent of the 47,000 supervisory jobs in a total Sears work force of 376,000. During the same period, the proportion of women in Sears's 3,000 professional jobs rose from 19.2 to 43.8 percent. The company's one-third ratio of women supervisors was three and a half times higher than the national average reported by the Office of Federal Contracts Compliance Programs (OFCCP) and more than twice as high as the 1974 average obtained from companies nationwide and reported by EEOC. However, the company made only modest progress in bringing women into crafts jobs, such as service technician and automotive mechanic, and neither Sears nor other firms succeeded in reducing the proportion of women (80 percent) among office and clerical workers.

Table 2: Changes in Proportions of Women and Minorities Employed by Sears and Firms Surveyed by the Office of Federal Contracts Compliance Programs, 1972 to 1975 (percent) [a]

Equal Employment Opportunity Categories	Women		Minorities	
	1972	1975	1972	1975
Officials and managers				
Sears	26.9	32.7	5.4	8.3
OFCCP firms	7.0	8.9	4.1	5.5
Office and clerical				
Sears	88.4	88.1	12.3	17.9
OFCCP firms	79.5	79.8	13.6	16.5
Crafts workers				
Sears	4.1	6.5	10.8	13.7
OFCCP firms	1.4	2.5	12.2	15.4

[a] OFCCP surveys 655 firms (federal contractors and subcontractors). The data in this table represent the averages for those firms.
Source: Sears, Roebuck and Company.

Between 1965 and 1976, Sears more than doubled the proportion of minority individuals in all jobs, from 8.7 to 18.9 percent, thereby exceeding the 18 percent minority representation in the national work force. Sears reports that in mid-1976, 8.8 percent of supervisors and 8.3 percent of professionals were minority individuals. These proportions were over 50 percent above the national averages reported by OFCCP for 1975. Sears also raised its proportion of minorities in crafts jobs from 6.4 to 14.8 percent. And although minority overrepresentation in blue-collar categories in general increased somewhat, Sears succeeded in decreasing this overrepresentation in the lowest-paid categories.

Special Training and Recruitment

Sears has found it difficult to overcome racial and sexual stereotyping in job placement. Progress has been very limited. Nevertheless, the company has undertaken a number of programs to rectify this situation.

Among its special efforts, Sears recruits male secretaries from among its employees and in high schools. The company emphasizes that secretaries are promotable into higher ranks. Sears's methodology is used to train women at the Bedford Hills Correctional Facility in New York State for jobs as automotive mechanics. The company expects to hire an average of seventy-five of these women each year. Sears donates tools and hardware, writes training manuals, and acts as a consultant to the Bedford Hills teaching staff.

Sears has a total of 800 store managers. At present, 35 of these managers are women or minority group members. Sears expects to double that number by 1979. However, because it takes ten years or more to develop a store manager, much depends on the number of qualified candidates progressing through the affirmative action program.

The Sears Minority Enterprise Small Business Investment Company, Tower Enterprises, is one of the most active in the country. (There are eighty such groups nationwide.) Since its inception in June 1975, the Sears group has made fourteen investments, totaling $1.2 million. Sears acts as an investment source of last resort for these minority-owned businesses and also buys many of their products, thus giving them an assured market.

Handicapped Workers

Depending on the size of the particular facility, from 3 to 11 percent of the employees of a Sears unit have some disability that would qualify them for state rehabilitation services. To facilitate and increase employment of the handicapped, the company established a program for the lessening and elimination of architectural barriers. In addition, it has made a survey of the work force and its unit managers to see whether accommodations are being made and whether company units are recruiting employees from rehabilitation agencies and sheltered workshops. The program is run by Paul L. Scher, head of the Selective Placement Program, who is a rehabilitation specialist and who is himself blind.

Evaluation of the Program

Sears estimates that it has spent $20 million overall during the last nine years on administration, data processing, research, recruitment, and management costs related to its affirmative action program. About $2 million of this was spent on responding to the EEOC charge in its 200-page *Request for Information.* These estimated costs are exclusive of extra training costs, such as those involved in nontraditional job training.

The company believes that it has chosen a wise approach to the problem. Graham explains that "top management realized that, whatever its problems might be, MAG was a key to attaining Sears's affirmative action goals and to dealing with continued underrepresentation in certain job categories. The voluntary approach means that we have more flexibility and control than we would have under a EEOC settlement and court decree. And it allows us to spread the costs over a greater number of years."

A crucial issue for Sears (and for thousands of large employers) is how the courts will treat affirmative action plans. Lee M. Finkel, a Sears attorney specializing in equal employment opportunity matters, points out the pressures on companies: "Government agencies and some courts seem to expect all employers to have achieved parity with the labor force or with the population composition in the area of company operations. But that view assumes that nonparity is the exclusive result of past or present discrimination. It does not take into consideration availability, interests, skills, and other relevant factors."

What course will the company take if MAG and other affirmative action systems are found to be illegal? Graham responds: "I think affirmative action programs would be emasculated if companies weren't given the leeway to force changes. Industry has been placed in the untenable position of having to show positive numerical results without resorting to systems that force the achievement of those results. I believe that the courts or Congress will have to resolve this issue."

STANDARD OIL OF CALIFORNIA

Hiring Vietnam Veterans and the Handicapped

Since 1971, Standard Oil of California (SOCAL) has listed all job openings with the local Employment Service offices in communities in which the company operates. This procedure is in compliance with a federal regulation designed to facilitate the employment of Vietnam veterans, including those who are disabled, and of qualified handicapped people.

The company reports that as a result, a minimum of 12 to 15 percent of its new employees each year have been Vietnam veterans. In 1972, which was a peak year, 500 of the 1,700 new hires (about 30 percent) were Vietnam veterans. During 1977, 12 percent of new hires were veterans. Of course, the proportion of veterans hired varies considerably according to the available job opportunities.

SOCAL employees may identify themselves as handicapped if they wish. However, Douglas Reid, SOCAL's affirmative action coordinator, reports that "very few, including visibly handicapped persons, have done so." He believes the reason for this is that disabled persons who are performing their jobs satisfactorily do not consider themselves handicapped.

"Our affirmative action program for employment of the handicapped has not been hard to sell internally," he says. "Employees at all levels have close friends or family members who are physically or mentally disabled. Consequently, efforts to alleviate the employment problems of the handicapped are well received. The main problem has been to find the job that best fits a particular handicapped person's qualifications and limitations from among those jobs open at the time he or she seeks employment."

Reid says that his department has not heard of any special mental or emotional problems that have affected the job performance of veterans or handicapped persons. He is convinced that the combination of greater corporate social awareness and government regulations has changed the outlook of many companies, encouraging the employment of such people.

Programs Aiding the Disadvantaged

A number of SOCAL's regular employee-relations activities benefit the disadvantaged. For example, almost 35 percent of the scholarships, graduate fellowships, and grants for professional study that the company sponsors are designated for members of minority groups and women. SOCAL employs college students in blue-collar, office, and professional-level summer jobs and in work-study positions. It also supports minority-owned businesses through purchases of goods and services, deposits in minority-owned banks, and placement of minority individuals in management positions at company-owned service stations.

SOCAL also gives financial support to community organizations that provide social services, job training, and placement assistance to the disadvantaged. In addition, SOCAL managers are personally involved in a number of these organizations through service as trustees, advisors, and volunteer counselors. Reid concludes that "this participation has resulted in better mutual understanding between groups that often have widely different economic beliefs and experiences."

WELLS FARGO BANK

A Customized Program for Upgrading Women and Minority Individuals

Wells Fargo Bank, which has its corporate headquarters in San Francisco, is the eleventh-largest bank in the nation; its 332 branches are located throughout California.

For many years, the bank has been engaged in a number of affirmative action programs, and it is proud of the results. As of June 1977, Wells Fargo employed 13,120 persons. Of this total, 4,105 (31.3 percent) were members of minority groups, and 9,089 (69.3 percent) were women. The most important area of equal opportunity concern is the category of officials, managers, and professionals. Of the 4,392 employees in this group in June 1977, 699 (15.9 percent) were minority individuals, and 1,923 (43.8 percent) were women.

"Most areas of the bank are now trying to recruit more minority and women MBAs," says Rosabella Safont, Wells Fargo's manager of employee development. "However, the competition with other companies is fierce. One of the goals of our chief officer, Richard Cooley, is to have fifty qualified and fully trained women branch managers by 1980."

To meet affirmative action goals and in some cases to make them feasible, the bank has applied various rapid career development programs over the last several years. One of the most successful programs, initiated in 1975, is Accelerated Career Development (ACD). ACD is a highly personalized approach to selecting and preparing women and minority bank officers for higher assignments. About thirty bank officers have so far taken part in ACD and been promoted through it. Most have been white women, but minority men and women have also participated.

ACD uses a training schedule developed by the candidate for promotion on the basis of the job's requirements and the candidate's evaluation of those areas in which he or she lacks sufficient knowledge or skills. Such individualized training allows candidates to learn at their own best speed. Even more important, it encourages the person to assume control of his or her own development. The custom-tailored features of ACD are innovative both for Wells Fargo's training programs and for affirmative action programs in general.

ACD procedures begin with an analysis that examines whole regional work force populations and points out job targets in which certain groups are inadequately represented. Division managers look for individual positions that will open up or can be created through expansion, and job grades, salaries, and responsibilities are listed for these positions. Potential candidates are identified among women and minorities. Eligibility is based on length of service and career movement, past performance, skills and knowledge, and personal job preferences. The top candidate is selected and asked whether he or she is willing to move into the new job category through ACD.

The candidate embarks on a series of interviews with bank officers who are already in that job class in order to learn what the major job responsibilities are; he or she may also talk to supervisors and subordinates. The candidate then summarizes the job tasks and compares them with his or her experience, taking into consideration technical skills, supervisory practices or other interpersonal skills.

On the basis of this information, a career-objective agreement is drawn up, mostly by the candidate, focusing on job content and personal development. This written agreement states what is expected, why, how training will be accomplished, when, and under whose guidance. In some cases, these agreements have been extremely detailed, citing long lists of job procedures to be learned. It also identifies one primary instructor and several other officers who will supervise the learning of specific skills. They, too, sign the agreement.

Once the agreement has been signed, the individual's training cycle begins. Each cycle takes approximately nine to twelve months, depending on the target job and the employee's assessment of his or her skills. The final phase of the cycle is a one-month simulation in which the candidate tries out the job without actually being responsible for that assignment. This tryout may be scheduled as a substitution for a bank officer who is on vacation or on assignment away from the branch. So far, however, more than half of the candidates have been assigned to their new jobs without going through the simulation stage.

Past ACD training cycles have included an orientation to the range of bank services, especially for branch manager candidates; a supervisory training program that concentrated on specific functions of the job, including the reports to be completed and what the division manager expects of supervisors; and an interpersonal-relations program for nonsupervisory personnel who were being accelerated to jobs that involve greater contact with the public.

"ACD provides a lot of individual attention," Safont says, "more than any other training program in the bank. It has been applied so far only to officers and only to the retail bank, in which more than half of our people work. However, we are beginning to rewrite the program in order to gain more commitment to it from our regional and divisional administrators. ACD has already served us well, indeed, as an instrument of affirmative action."

6 ALTERNATIVE WORK PATTERNS

INLAND STEEL COMPANY

Using a Four-Day Workweek to Reduce Layoffs

Because the steel industry is a cyclical business, downturns are inevitable. When Inland Steel's business turns sharply down, its first action is to stop hiring. Next, the big Midwest steel company reduces the schedules of a considerable number of employees to a four-day workweek. These shortened weeks are assigned on a fairly short, rotating basis. Only as a last resort does Inland turn to layoffs, and even then, any worker slated to be laid off is given the option of first taking any accrued vacation time.

Typically, the four-day workweek is instituted for two weeks at a time for any one group of employees. In addition, the reductions are spread among the company's various facilities so that not all those on reduced schedules work at the same mill. Inland has also avoided concentrating too much of a recession's ill effects at the company's huge steel mill in East Chicago, Indiana, which has produced more steel than any other mill in America over the last five years.

A major reason for Inland's use of this type of work sharing during recessions is that it is permitted by the United Steelworkers' contract with the companies. The agreement allows companies to implement the four-day workweek in order to avoid laying people off. Workers on the reduced schedules are not eligible for unemployment compensation, nor do they receive the Supplemental Unemployment Benefits provided by the steel and other industries. Of the 22,600 employees at the company's Indiana Harbor Works, only the 18,000 hourly workers are subject to layoffs. However, Inland Steel will make every effort to put hourly employees on the four-day workweek in order to avoid this possibility.

Statistics show how effective the reduced schedule has proved to be. The recent recession affected steel companies fairly late. Consequently, Inland's downturn was most severe in the fall of 1975. The week of October 8, 1975, was the company's worst. At that time, of the 18,000 hourly employees, Inland had 1,932 people on the four-day schedule and 569 workers on layoff.

The four-day week has been implemented during earlier recessionary periods, notably in 1971, when industrial customers built up huge inventories of steel in anticipation of a strike. Inland may use it during future downturns when the company does not have enough orders to run the mills at full capacity.

According to George Yoxall, Inland's manager of personnel and training, the four-day workweek has advantages for both the company and its employees. The company gains because the arrangement helps to keep work crews together and thus helps to maintain productivity. And even on the reduced week, employees can still earn a decent income because of the high steel industry wages.

As long as the shortened work schedules are in force for brief periods, the reduction in income is not serious. In 1975, Inland's minimum wage was $5 per hour, and the average was about $8 per hour, or $320 per week. When that was reduced by one-fifth ($64 a week), a worker still earned an average of $265 a week, or more than $1,000 a month. In addition, employees on the four-day week continue to receive full employee benefits.

MACY'S NEW YORK

Large Part-Time Work Force Serves Special Groups

Somewhat more than half of the 16,000 employees of Macy's New York, which comprises fifteen retail stores and three furniture outlets in the New York metropolitan area and suburbs, are part-timers. Their work schedules provide a degree of flexibility that is vital to the company and that also serves the special interests of a number of groups of employees, particularly women with families, retirees, and students.

Unlike most other industries, retail organizations are strongly dependent on part-time employees. Part-timers are especially prevalent in the retail sales force for two traditional reasons: First, retail stores are open for much longer hours than could be covered by any full-time work schedule. (Most Macy's stores are open from fifty-eight to seventy hours a week.) Second, salespeople must handle an uneven flow of customers. Heavy periods now include lunch and dinner hours, some evenings, Saturdays, and Sundays. And when customer traffic is heaviest, the sales force must be augmented.

Macy's suburban stores are open six nights a week (including Saturday) and, since September 1976, five hours on Sundays. To cover the Sunday staff needs, Macy's offered its employees the chance to swap one workday during the week for Sunday. However, the largest share of the work force needed for these extra hours has been filled by new hires; they are part-timers who work either Saturdays and Sundays or Sundays plus two or three evenings per week. In this process of expansion, Macy's has recruited a good mixture of part-time employees: a larger-than-average number of males and an even larger group of females, especially young mothers with preschoolers or school-age children.

Thus, part-time work is more than a tradition at Macy's. It is a growing trend.

Two Types of Part-Time Employees

Macy's employs two different types of part-timers: middle-of-the-day employees and short-hour employees. Although they reflect rather different working groups, they have certain characteristics in common. They are people who prefer not to work a full schedule or during conventional working hours, or they are people who have been unable to find full-time work with regular hours.

Together, the two groups total more than 8,000, or over half of the work force in the Macy's New York division. (The division constitutes roughly half of the company.) Presumably, the same proportions apply among Macy's workers elsewhere. At present, Macy's has more employees on short-hour schedules than on middle-of-the-day schedules. In the past, the proportions were about equal, but the addition of the Sunday hours tipped the balance toward short-hour employees.

Middle-of-the-day employees work five fixed days a week, usually from 12:00 to 5:00 P.M. on four days and from 1:00 to 9:00 P.M. on the fifth day. Others may work five mornings or five evenings, but those schedules are not typical. Thus, middle-of-the-day people regularly work between twenty-five and twenty-eight hours per week. Wage rates and benefits received by middle-of-the-day workers are identical to those of full-time employees. They are relatively well paid for retailing employees. The entry-level wage is $3.25 per hour, and eight labor grades and an array of occupations are available to them. Some raises are based on merit; others are given according to automatic step rates. The benefits package includes a health plan and a pension after twenty years. Part-timers must work 1,000 hours per year, or twenty hours per week, in order to qualify for a pension, as mandated by the Employee Retirement Income Security Act of 1974 (the federal pension law).

Short-hour employees work fewer than five days and often under twenty hours per week. They are mainly students, retirees, and moon-lighters; that is, they are typically the very young and the older workers. This group is much younger than the work force as a whole, and more of its members are male (although females still predominate).

The short-hour work force is not so stable as the middle-of-the-day group. Because students and retirees enter and leave the work force more frequently, the rate of turnover is higher. The wage rates are essentially the same as those paid to full-time employees, but because of their much shorter service, short-hour workers usually do not reach the higher wage brackets. Their fringe benefits are also more limited because many work at other jobs and receive benefits from their primary employer or are students who are covered by their parents' insurance policies.

Union Objections

Unions have often been unfriendly to the growing use of part-time workers. Union leaders have pointed out that benefits for part-timers are not always prorated, that part-timers may not have a strong commitment to union membership, and that it is often more difficult for a work force that is a mixture of full-time and part-time employees to agree on common nego-tiating goals if they have somewhat different interests and benefits.

Such union sensitivities affect Macy's as much as they do other retail chains, even though all part-time employees in unionized Macy's New York stores (six of the fifteen) are union members.

Exceptionally Stable Full-Time Work Force

Despite Macy's New York's increasing use of part-timers, its older full-time employees have proved to be an extraordinarily stable work force. There are 8,000 to 9,000 of them, and more than 1,200 (one-seventh of the full-time work force) have at least twenty-five years of service with the company.

Gertrude G. Michelson, senior vice president for personnel, explains why the company believes that the older work force is so stable: "Many of them came to work for us in the years shortly after the depression, when job mobility was so much lower. Also, there is the incentive in that our personnel policies are skewed toward long service; the benefits grow over the years. The personal lives of these employees have often been linked to the business. For example, they may have met spouses here, or their children may have been (or may now be) short-hour employees. These people take pride in staying with us. Such conditions don't apply nearly as much to younger employees."

A Tool for Retirement

Except in the case of its executive employees, Macy's imposes no mandatory retirement age. Therefore, part-time work is used by many employees as a means to stay on with the company and adjust to retirement. Some first-line supervisors have also requested to stay on a short-hours schedule. If management feels that they can handle the job, they are given part-time jobs as appropriate work becomes available.

How many employees stay on past age 64? Although up-to-date statistics are not available, Michelson says that "lots of people have availed themselves of the opportunity. But they usually don't stay at it very long," she explains. "After a year or two, they often find that they enjoy staying home more than they thought they would or that they can survive without the store. But it is a very important transition. It has tremendous emotional value."

Everyone Benefits

Older workers, housewives reentering the work force, students, and retirees all seem to be finding part-time employment eminently suited to their needs. Perhaps the largest group of part-timers is made up of women with very young and school-age children.

Macy's reports advantages to the company as well. The use of part-time employees offers the stores a better mix of males and females because it brings a greater number of younger males into an industry that has had a heavy overrepresentation of women, particularly in sales. Furthermore, the efficiency of using part-timers has been most fully developed in retailing. As Michelson points out, retailing, like many other fields that use part-timers, has a basic work load, but it also has regular, predictable peaks and valleys in the volume and timing of the total work load during which part-timers can be put to highly productive use.

Society as a whole also gains because many groups, such as students, retirees, and housewives, that traditionally show higher unemployment and lower work force participation rates, receive income through part-time work and thus become contributing, more productive citizens.

ZENITH RADIO CORPORATION

Learning on Layoff

During the first six months of 1975, the worst of the recession, about 1,000 of Zenith's 9,000 hourly employees in Chicago were laid off for an average of several months. However, fifty of these workers spent their layoffs in a six-month program, called Learning on Layoff, in which they studied basic and television electronics, basic mathematics, and reading, writing, and verbal communications. They received unemployment compensation plus a stipend of $1 per hour. All were volunteers, many of them women who desired a chance to upgrade their skills so that they would have opportunities for promotion. Most important, these workers kept their right to recall on a seniority basis. If they were recalled before completing their training, they could take educational leave to finish it.

This program fulfilled at least one purpose: Layoff time was used productively. But the Zenith Radio Corporation and the Chicago Mayor's Office of Manpower (MOM), the sponsors of Learning on Layoff, had two additional objectives: to prepare workers for better jobs and to enable the workers to carry out their present jobs more effectively if they were not promoted when recalled. Of the fifty participants, forty-eight were re-hired, and four were immediately promoted.

Zenith regards the program as a mixed success. "There weren't many opportunities for promotion in 1975," says Edward Youngman, personnel manager. "We don't know, however, if others were promoted later. For the workers, the payoff was to take advantage of additional education and to prepare for a better job. The problem was that although the program filled layoff time, there weren't enough promotions right after the program ended. For Zenith to undertake such a program again would depend on the resources." The training was carried out by the Continental Institute of Technology, a private Chicago company. Later in 1975, Continental received more city funds to train workers on layoff from Zenith and other companies; however, the funding was soon stopped, and Continental went out of business.

Work-related education is a regular activity at Zenith, costing several hundred thousand dollars per year in educational assistance from the employee-relations budget. Several hundred workers, out of 11,000 hourly and salaried employees in the Chicago area, take after-hours classes in English as a second language, electronics in the Spanish language, secretarial and clerical training (taken primarily by minority employees), and the high school equivalency degree (paid for in full by Zenith and taken after hours, outside the plant).

Thus, company policy has established a solid base for any future retraining program. And, in fact, Zenith already sponsors the variety of courses applicable to a much-enlarged program. However, neither the company nor the industry can presently offer much expansion in jobs.

Costs and Benefits

In a future recession, a CETA prime sponsor such as the city of Chicago would have to reconsider what benefits were attainable in relation to the costs.

The total program cost was $131,063, or $2,621 per trainee for six months. The government spent $110,000, and Zenith spent $21,063; in addition, unemployment benefits were paid. The program's cost to the government, $2,200 per student, was competitive with the cost of other government-supported training programs. However, although the television electronics industry, hard hit in recent years by rising import competition, was able to rehire workers on layoff, promotions and transfers were restricted.

In a recessionary job market, it might be preferable to apply work sharing through a four-day or three-day workweek. But Zenith's union contracts preclude applying a shortened schedule for any extended period. "Ours is all or none," Youngman explains. "The junior employees get bumped. We have spread work by shutting down for a week to two, and in the spring and fall of 1975, we went to a three-day or a four-day workweek briefly, but only twice that year."

Effect of the Economy

Samuel Bernstein, head of MOM, points out that General Electric experienced similar results in using a community college to train some of its Chicago workers who were on layoff. "Very few were called back to higher-paying jobs. They went back to their old jobs. The concept was great. Here were workers who would have vegetated on unemployment insurance. Instead, they were motivated to improve themselves. Here was one alternative to layoffs, we thought: linking unemployment benefits to training programs."

Bernstein calculates that the Zenith and GE projects "cost one-third of what the normal government-funded training programs cost. After all, we didn't have to pay training allowances; these were waived because the workers were drawing unemployment insurance. Otherwise, these allowances make up two-thirds of the cost of a training program."

However, the goal of the program was higher-paying jobs, not just better-trained workers. "The only problem was that we guessed wrong; the electronics industry didn't turn up as we expected. If the economy and the industry had burgeoned then, this Zenith program would have been an example for the nation."

"The whole assumption," Bernstein concludes, "is that the jobs are out there and that we should act wherever there is a lack of trained people to fill the jobs. But this means that occupational forecasting based on accurate data is imperative. Nevertheless, at least we have taken individuals who had no opportunity to compete and given them one."

About CED

The Committee for Economic Development is composed of approximately two hundred trustees, most of whom are presidents or board chairmen of major corporations or university presidents. With the help of advisory boards made up of distinguished scholars and a small professional staff, the trustees work together to conduct research and formulate policy recommendations on major economic issues and to promote an understanding of the operation of the American economy. CED's policy statements are issued by its Research and Policy Committee, which is composed of approximately sixty trustees.

CED's objectives are to contribute to preserving and strengthening our free society, achieving steady economic growth at high employment and reasonably stable prices, increasing productivity and living standards, providing greater and more equal opportunity for every citizen, and improving the quality of life for all.

CED's bylaws emphasize that its work must be thoroughly objective in character and that each issue must be approached, not from the viewpoint of any particular economic or political group, but from that of the general welfare.

CED is supported by contributions from business and industry, foundations, and individuals. It is nonprofit, nonpartisan, and nonpolitical.

About WORK IN AMERICA INSTITUTE

Work in America Institute is a nonprofit, nonpartisan organization founded in 1975 to advance productivity and the quality of working life. It has a broad base of participation from business, unions, government agencies, foundations, universities, and research institutes, both in the United States and abroad. Through its programs, the Institute provides organized and continuing support to all sectors of the work community in its efforts to motivate the work force toward higher achievement and self-esteem in their working lives and to promote a vital economic system.

The Institute provides technical assistance and analysis, communications, and clearinghouse services to business and public and private organizations.

The Institute draws its support from corporations, labor unions, government agencies, and foundations.

CED Research and Policy Committee

Chairman
FRANKLIN A. LINDSAY

Vice Chairmen
JOHN L. BURNS / *Education and Social and Urban Development*

E. B. FITZGERALD / *International Economy*

HOWARD C. PETERSEN / *National Economy*

WAYNE E. THOMPSON / *Improvement of Management in Government*

A. ROBERT ABBOUD, Chairman
The First National Bank of Chicago
SANFORD S. ATWOOD
Lake Toxaway, North Carolina
JOSEPH W. BARR
Washington, D.C.
HARRY HOOD BASSETT, Chairman
Southeast Banking Corporation
JACK F. BENNETT
Senior Vice President
Exxon Corporation
CHARLES P. BOWEN, Jr.
Honorary Chairman
Booz, Allen & Hamilton Inc.
JOHN L. BURNS, President
John L. Burns and Company
FLETCHER L. BYROM, Chairman
Koppers Company, Inc.
ROBERT J. CARLSON
Senior Vice President
Deere & Company
RAFAEL CARRION, JR.
Chairman and President
Banco Popular de Puerto Rico
WILLIAM S. CASHEL, JR.
Vice Chairman
American Telephone & Telegraph Company
JOHN B. CAVE, Senior Vice President,
    Finance and Administration
Schering-Plough Corporation
EMILIO G. COLLADO, President
Adela Investment Co., S.A.
ROBERT C. COSGROVE, Chairman
Green Giant Company
JOHN H. DANIELS, Chairman
National City Bancorporation
W. D. EBERLE, Special Partner
Robert A. Weaver, Jr. and Associates
FRANCIS E. FERGUSON, President
Northwestern Mutual Life
Insurance Company
JOHN H. FILER, Chairman
Aetna Life and Casualty Company
E.B. FITZGERALD, Chairman
Cutler-Hammer, Inc.
JOHN M. FOX, Retired Chairman
H. P. Hood Inc.

DAVID L. FRANCIS
Chairman and President
Princess Coals, Inc.
WILLIAM H. FRANKLIN
Chairman of the Board (Retired)
Caterpillar Tractor Co.
JOHN D. GRAY, Chairman
Omark Industries, Inc.
TERRANCE HANOLD
Minneapolis, Minnesota
H. J. HEINZ II, Chairman
H. J. Heinz Company
ROBERT C. HOLLAND, President
Committee for Economic Development
GILBERT E. JONES
Retired Vice Chairman
IBM Corporation
EDWARD R. KANE, President
E. I. du Pont de Nemours & Company
CHARLES KELLER, JR.
New Orleans, Louisiana
JAMES R. KENNEDY
Essex Fells, New Jersey
PHILIP M. KLUTZNICK
Klutznick Investments
RALPH LAZARUS, Chairman
Federated Department Stores, Inc.
FRANKLIN A. LINDSAY, Chairman
Itek Corporation
G. BARRON MALLORY
Jacobs Persinger & Parker
THOMAS B. McCABE
Chairman, Finance Committee
Scott Paper Company
GEORGE C. McGHEE
Corporate Director and
    Former U.S. Ambassador
Washington, D.C.
E. L. McNEELY, Chairman
The Wickes Corporation
J. W. McSWINEY, Chairman
The Mead Corporation
ROBERT R. NATHAN, President
Robert R. Nathan Associates, Inc.
HOWARD C. PETERSEN, Chairman
The Fidelity Bank

C. WREDE PETERSMEYER
Retired Chairman
Corinthian Broadcasting Corporation
R. STEWART RAUCH, JR.
Chairman
The Philadelphia Saving Fund Society
JAMES Q. RIORDAN
Executive Vice President
Mobil Oil Corporation
MELVIN J. ROBERTS
Colorado National Bankshares, Inc.
WILLIAM M. ROTH
San Francisco, California
HENRY B. SCHACHT, Chairman
Cummins Engine Company, Inc.
ROBERT B. SEMPLE, Chairman
BASF Wyandotte Corporation
ROCCO C. SICILIANO, Chairman
TICOR
ROGER B. SMITH
Executive Vice President
General Motors Corporation
CHARLES B. STAUFFACHER
President
Field Enterprises, Inc.
WILLIAM C. STOLK
Weston, Connecticut
WALTER N. THAYER, President
Whitney Communications Corporation
WAYNE E. THOMPSON
Senior Vice President
Dayton Hudson Corporation
J. W. VAN GORKOM, President
Trans Union Corporation
SIDNEY J. WEINBERG, JR., Partner
Goldman, Sachs & Co.
GEORGE L. WILCOX
Director-Officer
Westinghouse Electric Corporation
FRAZAR B. WILDE
Chairman Emeritus
Connecticut General Life Insurance
    Company

Subcommittee on Employment
for the Young, Old, Disadvantaged, and Displaced

Training and Jobs Programs in Action:
Case Studies in Private-Sector Initiatives
for the Hard-to-Employ

Related Materials

Please write to CED for information on other publications and materials on jobs for the hard-to-employ.

"Jobs for the Hard-to-Employ: New Directions for a Public-Private Partnership"

This policy statement calls for a renewed public and private commitment to reducing structural unemployment without inflation. Calls for stronger organizational mechanisms to mobilize the private sector and new and expanded use of programs that already work.

Review and Discussion Guide: "Jobs for the Hard-to-Employ"

Designed to stimulate discussion and debate on the issues raised in the CED policy satement.

Digest: "Jobs for the Hard-to-Employ"

A pocket-size summary of the key issues and major recommendations contained in the CED policy statement.

Filmstrip: "Jobs for the Hard-to-Employ"

A 14-minute color filmstrip with synchronized sound track explaining key issues covered in the CED policy statement.

COMMITTEE FOR ECONOMIC DEVELOPMENT
477 Madison Avenue, New York, N. Y. 10022   (212) 688-2063

DATE DUE

DEMCO 38-297